Midland Rivers

by John Drewett and John Roberts

The geography, history, character, plants and creatures
of the great rivers of the Midlands - Trent, Severn and Avon,
and their main tributaries.

****
Quercus
John Roberts
8 Hillside Close, Bartley Green
Birmingham B32 4LT
****

Midland Rivers
by John Drewett and John Roberts

ISBN 1 898136 08 4

First Published 1996

The Wildlife Trusts
in the Heart of England

The environment is our most important and precious asset. The West Midlands, the Heart of England, is a region of great natural diversity with a rich variety of wildlife.

The five Wildlife Trusts which cover the region have been caring for wildlife for more than 25 years. Together they manage more than 100 nature reserves, from the wild and windswept moors of north Staffordshire to the gentle and pastoral river valleys of Worcestershire. They collect and disseminate information about the region's wildlife and campaign for its protection.

The task is enormous and is impossible without your help. You could join your local Wildlife Trust, help manage a local nature reserve or organise a fund raising event. To find out more, contact your nearest Wildlife Trust today.

Shropshire Wildlife Trust
Shropshire Wildlife
Conservation Centre
167 Frankwell
Shrewsbury
SY3 8LG
Tel (0743) 241691

Staffordshire Wildlife Trust
Coutts House
Sandon
Stafford
ST18 0DN
Tel (0889) 508534

Urban Wildlife Trust
Unit 310
Jubilee Trades Centre
130 Pershore Street
Birmingham
B5 6ND
Tel (021) 666 7474

Warwickshire Wildlife Trust
Brandon Marsh Nature Centre
Brandon Lane
Coventry
CV3 3GW
Tel (0926) 496848

Worcestershire Nature
Conservation Trust
Lower Smite Farm
Smite Hill
Worcester
WR3 8SZ
Tel (0905) 754919

Caring for Wildlife
IN THE HEART OF ENGLAND

The Authors

JOHN DREWETT was born in Horsham, West Sussex and grew up in Box Hill, Surrey among the wooded hills and valleys of The Weald. Wildlife became an interest when he was young and spent his spare time walking the downs, woods and heaths of the county.

Working first in insurance, John developed his interest in wild creatures, plants and conservation, and he spent many hours in voluntary work with the Surrey Wildlife Trust. In 1986 he became a Development Officer with the Staffordshire Wildlife Trust. Now living in Yorkshire, he works as a freelance writer on environment and travel topics.

John has written on wildlife and the countryside in many publications including Country Life, Yorkshire Post, The Lady and the Aberdeen Press & Journal. He has a weekly wildlife column in the Stafford Post and has written two books about Surrey. With John Roberts he wrote another Quercus book, *Midland Woods & Forests*. He likes walking, reading and archaeology.

JOHN ROBERTS was born a very long time ago and grew up on the Wirral. His early playgrounds were the Cheshire woods and lanes. He has since lived on the Lancashire coast, near Lichfield, on the edge of Stourbridge and in Birmingham. All but two of his eight homes have been on the edges of towns so walking and the landscape have always been part of his life.

John worked in insurance and served time as a Loss Adjuster, then became a lecturer in insurance and law. He started writing and publishing walks in his spare time, and after some years developing the WALKWAYS imprint, he turned to full time publishing. Soon after he launched Quercus, which will focus on Midland themes with many titles about the countryside.

John Drewett wrote the basic text and all the expert bits. John Roberts added material on navigation, water supply etc, with observations on the views and lots of boring details.

The cast iron Victorian road bridge over the Avon at Hampton Lucy

Stourport Basin by the Severn

Contents

Introduction

This book is a description of the main rivers in the western Midlands.
You will already know something about the Severn, the Avon and the
Trent, but may never have heard of the Salwarpe and Swarbourn. We
hope to provide you with some new knowledge and show the part they
play in the region, the problems they can cause, their fascination
and the joy they can give.

Each river has its own character and together they have shaped the
history and development of the Midlands. The Avon is a meandering
lowland river which waters rich farmland and market gardens. The
Trent is generally broad and direct, and with its urban tributary the
Tame, serves industry. The upper reaches of the Severn flow in deep,
steep valleys through green sheep country; further south it becomes
a more powerful cousin of the Avon. Burton is not "on Trent", nor
Stratford "upon Avon" for no reason. There were good reasons for
building power stations by the Trent and devloping metal forging
along the Stour in the Black Country. You will find some rivers
clean and full of life, others are polluted and awash with litter,
shopping trolleys and old bikes.

The three main rivers have sections of their own. We have selected
from the smaller rivers and included those with interesting features.
In a lifetime we could have found out something interesting about
every tiny stream, but we felt sure you could not wait, so we have
said what we felt was needed to describe the rivers as a system.
This book is a full introduction but not a collection of detailed
surveys. To find out more, start with the Reading List.

We describe the rivers from source to mouth, but as you will see
in *Landscape with Rivers* below, this book is about the river system
in what geographers call the Midland Triangle. Many rivers have
both ends outside it, so in those cases we have concentrated on the
stretch within our area but given a full outline of the rest. After
the opening sections the book falls into three main parts dealing
with the Severn, Avon and Trent and their tributaries.

The maps are sketches to an approximate scale and we claim no great
accuracy for them. They are illustrations showing main features which
we hope help to explain the river system, but there is no way in which
we could have depicted every detail that we mention. For more detail

and greater accuracy you must turn to the Ordnance Survey Landranger maps, though you would need rather a lot to cover all the rivers. Here we list the main rivers and tributaries and relevant map sheets. Other rivers mentioned can also be found on these maps. Alternatively, good quality atlases are available which cover the ground quite adequately at much less cost.

River Severn: Newtown & Llanidloes 136, Shrewsbury 126, Stafford & Telford, 127 Kidderminster & Wyre Forest 138, Worcester & the Malverns 150.

River Tern: Stafford & Telford 127, Shrewsbury 126.

River Stour (Black Country): Birmingham 139, Kidderminster & Wyre Forest 138.

River Teme: Newtown & Llanidloes 136, Ludlow & Wenlock Edge 137, Worcester & the Malverns 150.

River Avon: Leicester & Coventry 140, Stratford upon Avon 151, Worcester & the Malverns 150.

River Sowe: Leicester & Coventry 140.

River Leam: Stratford upon Avon 151.

River Stour: Stratford upon Avon 151.

River Arrow: Birmingham 139, Stratford upon Avon 151.

River Trent: Stoke on Trent & Macclesfield 118, Stafford & Telford 127, Derby & Burton on Trent 128.

River Sow: Stafford & Telford 127.

River Blithe: Stoke on Trent & Macclesfield 118, Stafford & Telford 127, Derby & Burton on Trent 129.

River Tame: Birmingham 139, Derby & Burton on Trent 128.

River Dove: Buxton & Matlock 119, Derby & Burton on Trent 128.

We must give our sincere thanks to the dedicated people who have studied and protected our rivers over the years. Much of our material is based on their discoveries and records. Special thanks to the National Rivers Authority and the various Wildlife Trusts who let us study their files and answered many questions. We have visited all the rivers in the book, but in spite of many days splashing and squelching it could not have been written without those workers.

Misty winter Severn near Northwick just upstream of Worcester

"They're playing our play." - The Avon at Stratford

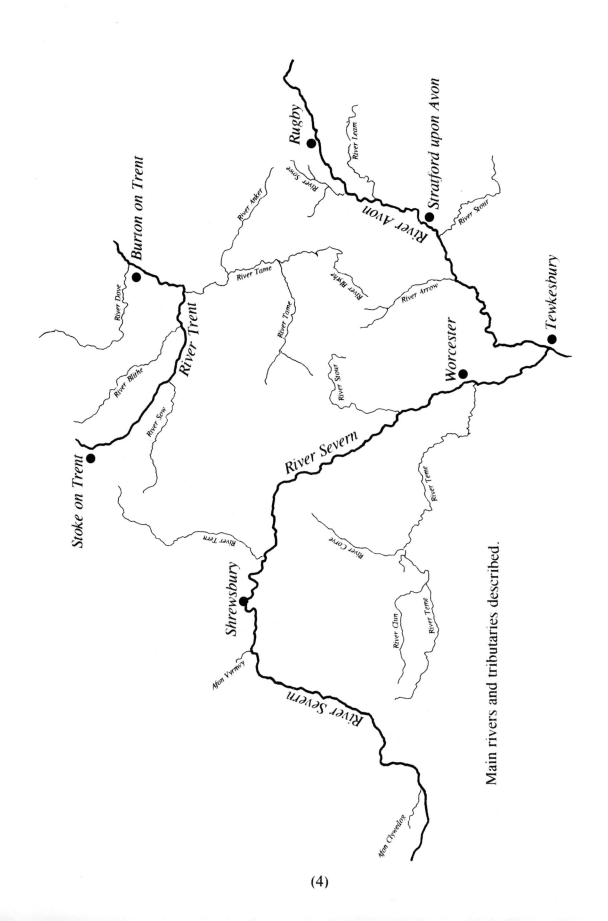

Main rivers and tributaries described.

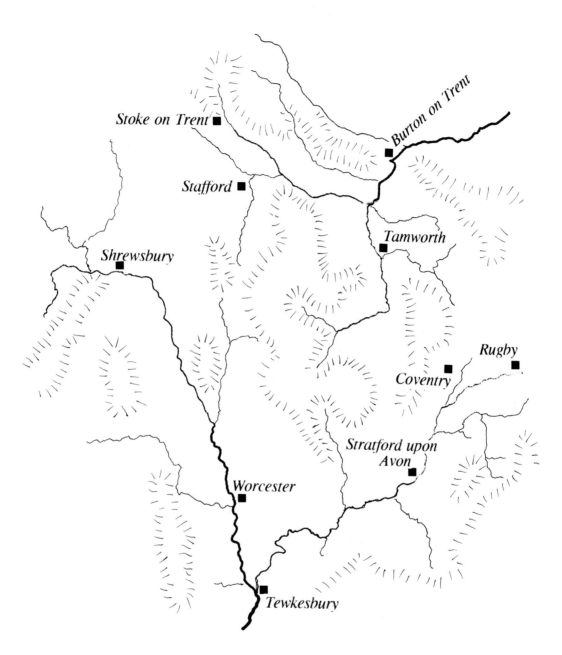

Stoke on Trent

Burton on Trent

Stafford

Tamworth

Shrewsbury

Rugby

Coventry

Stratford upon
Avon

Worcester

Tewkesbury

Main rivers and land
over about 125 metres.

Landscape with Rivers

In this introduction to the landscape of the "Midlands Triangle", as geographers call it, it was clearly, sadly inevitable that we would have to say very much the same things as we did in *Midland Woods & Forests*. Readers are asked to forgive us, since we have tried to find new cliches and hyperbole.

The map shows that the region is indeed a rough triangle. The western edge is much higher than the rest. Wenlock Edge reaches about 339 metres, the Clee Hills 546, the Abberley Hills further south about 280, and the Malverns 425 metres. The southern rim has large gaps across the plains of the Severn and Avon. They are partly blocked by Breedon Hill (290 metres), the northern edge of the Cotswolds with intermittent high points between 240 and 280 metres, and Edge Hill (227 metres). The east side has a gap which is blocked by the hills at Nuneaton and Atherstone. Although only 170 metres high, they rise so steeply from the level plain which dissolves into Leicestershire that they are just as important as the western hills. They form the eastern edge of a block which reaches 184 metres at Corley Moor. From it, a broken chain of small hills leads south-wards towards Meriden.

In the north-east there is a big gap across the plain of the Trent, but just to the north the low hills of east Staffordshire reach 160 metres. Across the north side of the triangle is the flat green landscape between Trent and Severn, miles of undulating fields until the ground rises towards The Wrekin and Wenlock Edge.

Down the centre of this great saucer runs a broken block of higher ground from Cannock Chase in the north, through Walsall and Birmingham, and west to the Severn. In the east there is a steady fall towards the River Tame and a slope towards Coventry, but the plateau has a distinct southern edge at Tardebigge, near Bromsgrove, and Knowle south of Solihull. A long ridge continues south to Redditch and Alcester, where you are close to the northern edge of the Vale of Evesham.

High points in this central plateau include Castle Ring on Cannock Chase at 244 metres. Beacon Hill in Walsall at 227, Kinver Edge west of Stourbridge at 166 metres, with the Clent and Lickey Hills south of Birmingham at 315 and 291 metres.

The lowlands in this saucer are the plains of the three main rivers, Trent, Severn and Avon, and their tributaries. The geographers refer to three "gates" out of the Midland Triangle. By the Severn Gate the Severn and Avon head south, the Trent Gate is to the east. The Midland Gate is a broad plain across south Staffordshire and north east Shropshire which is drained by two Trent bound rivers, the Penk and the Sow, and two Severn tributaries, the Tern and Roden.

Down the western side of the region the Severn flows within a narrow gorge at Ironbridge, the craggy, limestone northern end of Wenlock Edge. Further south past Bridgnorth and Bewdley the river stays between steep banks. Only south of Stourport does it start to form a recognisable plain, though still deep in its banks to Worcester.

At Tewkesbury the Severn is joined by the Warwickshire Avon. For most of its length the Avon winds and meanders past Rugby, Coventry, Leamington, Warwick and Stratford, collecting equally absent minded tributaries such as the Arrow, the Leam and the Stour. Their broad, shallow valleys cover a great deal of mid Warwickshire.

The Trent valley is the broadest and flattest of the three, and its tributaries range furthest. The Tame rises near Wolverhampton and with the Cole, the Rea and lesser streams it drains the Birmingham plateau. The Anker flows past Nuneaton to Tamworth. North and west of Cannock Chase, the Sow and Penk trickle off the even landscape north and north-west of Wolverhampton. Their drainage systems cover most of south Staffordshire and north-east Shropshire.

Scenery and rivers are formed by the ground on which they lie. Hills, ridges and valleys, their height and steepness, affect and reflect soil types and depths, as well as the speed and character of the rivers.

Rocks from most geological periods can be found in the Midlands. Near Atherstone and at Rowley Regis are the most ancient igneous (volcanic) rocks and there are Precambrian fragments at Barnt Green and Lilleshall. But most rocks nearest the surface are sedimentary, formed from the mud and ooze in the beds of ancient estuaries and seas. Since the water left its deposits, they have been parched, windblown, flooded and washed, raised, lowered and cracked.

High points on the western side of the triangle are Old Red Sandstone, which is hard and resists erosion. The rest of the area is underlain by New Red Sandstone, except for the limestone of Wenlock Edge.

There are three general types of surface rock and therefore soil in the area. In the south and south-west, from where the Severn forms a plain, and across through Evesham and Rugby to Leicester, is Lias Clay. The other plains are Marl, or clay with rocks, which is on the whole rather alkaline. It makes a level and monotonous landscape but the scenery is improved by occasional sandstone outcrops.

Some ten thousand years ago the latest major geological event resolved itself as the great glaciers melted and dumped their burden of rubble. This treasure of rocks and pebbles had been gouged from north and east England, Wales and Scotland. The result is a variety of soils in the Midlands from the pebbly ground of Cannock Chase, the sand to the west and south of the West Midlands conurbation and the deep loam of the Vale of Evesham.

These vast dumps of glacial debris had a profound effect on the rivers. In many places they blocked their valleys forming great lakes. These submerged mile after mile of landscape until they overflowed the rim of land which contained them and cut deep channels like the Ironbridge Gorge. The rivers never resumed their original course. If they had, the Severn would not be in this book.

The melting of the ice was not the end of the Ice Age. Britain has been in *an* Ice Age for millions of years. Over that time there have been numerous glaciations (cold periods) and interglacials (not quite so cold). As they come and go, so do the ice sheets. Geologists tell us that we are currently enjoying an interglacial and global warming or not, one day there will be another freeze.

You could hardly get further from the British coast than the Midlands, but our rivers and streams give a direct link with both North and Irish Seas. Some of the water from every shower that falls on the Midlands finds its way to the sea. Some splashes straight into rivers and streams. Most of it falls on land where it either flows over the surface towards the nearest watercourse, or seeps into the soil. From here it will eventually find its way into drains and to a river, or be stored as groundwater. Part of this will eventually be released through springs and trickle towards the rivers.

Depending on just where in the region it falls, some of this water will reach the Bristol Channel via the River Severn. The rest will make it to the North Sea down the Trent and Humber. All other rivers and streams in the region feed into these two great rivers, the longest and the third longest rivers in Great Britain.

The basic factor which decides which way water flows is the topography of the land. The ridge which divides two catchment areas is the watershed, and on the map we have shown the main Midland watersheds between Severn and Trent. The word *ridge* suggests mountains or at least hills, but a watershed can be an insignificant hump in a level landscape.

The tiny hamlet of Whitley Heath is just off the A519 between Eccleshall and Woodseaves in Staffordshire. On the north side of the road a tiny stream begins life in a field. This is the Lonco Brook, which joins the River Tern, itself a tributary of the Severn. Less than three hundred yards away on the other side of the road, another stream trickles across a field. First called Clanford Brook, as it meets other streams it grows, becoming Doxey Brook then the River Sow and meeting the Trent at Shugborough. You can barely detect any slope between the two sources.

In Wolverhampton, the Smestow Brook surfaces near the racecourse and flows through the suburbs beside the Staffordshire & Worcestershire Canal. Leaving the conurbation it flows into the River Stour near Kinver, which heads for the Severn. In a lake at Perton just over a mile from the course of the Smestow Brook, the River Penk is born. It heads off in a north-easterly direction, passing around the northern edge of Cannock Chase to reach the Trent.

Rivers and streams do many jobs. They drain the land and carry excess water to the sea. They are vital habitats to a vast range of wildlife. They supply water to millions of people across the region, at the same time carrying away their sewage and dirty water. They provide power and water to industry and vast amounts of cooling water to power stations.

It is no coincidence that the main water supply company for the Midlands is Severn Trent Water. When the statutory water authorities were formed in England and Wales, the areas they served were made to coincide with water catchment areas. This logic was preserved during privatisation, so that now both the company and the pollution watchdog, the National Rivers Authority, base their structure on this natural geographic area.

The rivers of the Midlands underpin the whole of the life and economy of the region. Their future and ours depends on sensitive management and care, and we can only give that if we understand them.

Rivers at Work

Rivers are drains. They may inspire musicians, poets, lovers, fish and herons, but the reason for and the cause of their existence is that they carry water from higher to lower places. This essential feature gives them all their value and is the cause of all the trouble they cause for human beings.

Rivers drain the land and sometimes cause floods, but that is not all. They supply water for drinking, industry and irrigation, they dispose of wastes, they allow easy transport of heavy loads, they can be induced to release their colossal energy to power machines, they may provide food and often give recreation. And just as important as any of these, rivers and their banks provide habitat for a wide range of plants and creatures which are interesting and give pleasure, but are also essential to a balanced and healthy environment.

Midland rivers have been used and abused by people for countless centuries. From the earliest prehistoric times when they provided drinking water for settlers they have been part of the human way of life. In those days there were too few people for pollution to be a serious problem.

In those early times rivers were not only one of life's essentials, they also formed boundaries. Large rivers like the Severn and Trent were difficult to cross. For thousands of years the Trent was the boundary between north and south. Gradually, with the development of bridges, rivers became less of a barrier, though even today there are relatively few places where you can cross the lower reaches of the Severn.

The tailrace boils out of Hampton Lucy Mill on the Avon

In the following sections we will say something about each of the major functions of the Midland rivers such as drainage (natural, domestic and industrial), water supply, natural habitat, and recreation. It becomes obvious that these functions are incompatible and that if the rivers are to carry on performing them, strict controls to balance these uses are essential. We therefore start by outlining the present system of ownership and control.

Ownership & control

Rivers are owned by their "riparian owners", meaning that anyone who has a freehold in land beside a river also holds the bed as far as the middle. This may be subject to a public right of navigation, which is rather like a public right of way across a farm. The riparian owner owns trees or plants growing in the water, but not the water itself or the fish. In fact nobody owns wild fish any more than they own the wild birds on their land. The freeholder may of course lease the land, and therefore the river to a tenant. Riparian ownership includes the right to fish the river, subject to an NRA licence, and this right can be leased with the land or separately. There may be a right to abstract water, but only if it was being taken in 1930. Otherwise, ownership of a river has similar restrictions as holding any other piece of land. Buildings or structures require permission from the Planning Authority and the NRA, the owner is not free to discharge effluent into the river, obstruct navigation, abstract water or alter the banks.

The public interest in rivers has always been large and obvious. Owners have not been free for centuries to impede navigation, divert the flow or pollute as they wished. The rules may have been inadequate and unsystematic. In the cases of flood control and pollution, the subjects were imperfectly understood and the remedies often beyond the technical resources of society. Without modern administrative and policing systems the laws were difficult to enforce. But they did exist and demonstrate the central place of rivers in the economy.

The public law governing rivers is now found in the Water Resources Act 1991 which replaced earlier Acts. They established and laid duties on the National Rivers Authority (NRA) and gave powers to carry them out, such as to licence, investigate problems and prosecute offenders.

Drinking water is covered by the same Act which established the various (now private) water supply companies and OFWAT, the state body which regulates them. We are not concerned with drinking water as such in this book, though here and there we refer to its storage and abstraction.

Navigation of the rivers and canals is controlled in the Midlands by British Waterways Board and the Upper and Lower Avon Navigation Trusts. Their function is to maintain the rivers in a navigable state and to control and license traffic.

The NRA is responsible for protecting and improving all sources and reserves of water, rivers, streams and ditches, springs and underground supplies, lakes and ponds. They also cover estuaries and the sea up to six miles from the coast.

Their duties and powers are to control pollution, manage land drainage and flood protection, fisheries, drinking and industrial water supplies, conservation and recreation. We can hardly exagerate the importance of the NRA, which should emerge in the section on *Pollution & River Conservation*. We can give only the barest outline of the scope and complexity of their work, but please look at the section, *Further Reading*, where we list some of their pamphlets.

In 1994 the Government announced that the National Rivers Authority and Her Majesty's Inspectorate of Pollution would be merged in 1996. Preliminary notices suggested that whilst there was some logic in combining land and water pollution control functions, the brief for the new organisation (the Environment Agency) would weaken NRA work towards conserving and improving wildlife habitats.

Press releases from Friends of the Earth between August and November 1994 refer to previous cuts in NRA and HMIP funding and further cuts likely to follow the merger. The heads of both the agencies had been complaining and warning against this trend. One release in November comments on NRA plans to let water companies police the effluents from their own sewage works, which seems very likely to be a consequence of funding cuts.

Conservationists were sceptical about the ability of the NRA to promote conservation when it was founded, but were proved wrong. Indeed, in their 1994 press comment Friends of the Earth acknowledged progess. It may well be that the Government is being influenced by interests who find such progress expensive. However we hope as we imagine do FoE, that they will be wrong again this time.

Drainage & flood control

Drainage, we have said, is the main natural function of rivers. When they are having to accept more water than they can cope with they may, temporarily, have to dump some of it until they have disposed of water downstream. Usually they overflow onto known flood plains, so the River Severn spreads across the flatter parts of Shropshire and near Tewsksbury. Where more or less regular flooding is expected people do not build, and the farmers can cope with and even benefit from the flush of silt. So flood control is carried out to protect property in places where a river might more occasionally overtop its normal channel. It is an attempt to cause the river to perform its main task more efficiently.

However, drainage is not a river's only function and if we concentrate too hard on efficiency (as we see it) in one task, we may impair its ability to perform others.

It is strange that we now spend so much effort keeping floods off the land. The National Rivers Authority, and the Severn Trent Water Authority before them, are charged with the duty of flood prevention. Taking the traditional and narrow view of efficiency, this has often resulted in a policy which sends water downstream to the sea as fast as possible. It is true that we have been steadily draining our landscape for the last four centuries, but some of the most intensive efforts have been made since the 1950's. For the conservation of the river environment, it has serious implications.

In the past the land of Great Britain was very much wetter than it is now. The East Anglian Fens, the Somerset Levels, the Essex Marshes, Lancashire Mosses and Severn Lowlands were not neatly farmed fields with well manicured ditches, but treacherous and terrifying swamps. At Henley in Arden in Warwickshire there was a big marsh. Beside the River Leam above Leamington Spa and at Princethorpe was marsh. In these places malaria was endemic and probably this is what most "plagues and agues" were. For many people life must have been miserable for many months of the year, to be followed by a short and arthritic old age.

The Romans carried out many drainage and flood control works in East Anglia, but it was after 1600 that we made serious efforts to drain and dry the country. Steadily, with increasing wealth available to pay for works, with improvements in methods of drainage and enclosure of common land encouraging the trend, ditches were deepened and rivers

The Severn in flood at Atcham

Sluice gates above Stanford reservoir on the Avon

widened. In 1764 at Princethorpe, Warwickshire Joseph Elkington was fed up with his sheep suffering footrot. He had been trying to dry out his land using surface drains and was getting nowhere. One day, in exasperation, he thrust an iron bar vertically into a ditch and was rewarded by a great geyser of water. Elkington had intercepted a spring and very quickly established techniques of under drainage. He made a fortune by supplying clay drainage tiles to farmers, the principles are the same today.

General drainage became more widespread and techniques improved over the nineteenth century, for example by the use of steam pumps. Some people began to notice that the effects of drainage were not entirely beneficial. The rural poet John Clare and the artist and designer William Morris protested about the destruction of beautiful scenes. On the Fens, drainage since Roman times was shrinking the land itself, and surface levels have now fallen several metres, ironically increasing the danger of flooding from the sea. However, environmental concerns were usually treated lightly and carried little weight in a society in love with the optimistic, human centred, technologically based ideas of permanent "progress", "improvement" and "growth" through mastering nature.

During World War II agriculture was revived after decades of stagnation, to grow for us food which could no longer be easily imported from the Commonwealth. The drive for increased farm production (and this is a staggering fact) totally dominated landscape and countryside issues for the next fifty years. The policies adopted made it profitable to eliminate many farm ponds, grub out hedges and to drain more land, causing greater run off to the rivers and more silt. Elsewhere we discuss some of the other effects of this farm centred approach; nasty new effluents from silage making and slurry ponding, and the tonnes of nitrate fertilisers washed down into rivers. Only in the 1980s' was the extortionate cost of the EU farm support budget questioned, to begin a revision of aims and a series of adjustments which continue.

Other developments in society were contributing to the draining of the land and increased run-off into the rivers. New roads, airports, housing and industrial developments create impervious surfaces which keep rain out of the land beneath and shoot it down the drains. At the same time, some of this new property was on low lying land and increased the demand for flood protection. In the early 1970s an enormous amount of river engineering was carried out to prevent flooding. To appreciate its impact on the environment you will need to use your imagination.

Think of a river lined by willows, alders and the other trees of wet places. As it meanders through the gentle rises and falls of the Midland landscape, kingfishers, wagtails, moorhens and warblers make it their home. The banks are lined with wild flowers; purple loosestrife, marsh marigold, yellow flag - and with reeds, mosses and liverworts. A water vole perched dangerously on a fallen branch in the water feeds on some vegetation; as you approach he plops into the water and out of sight. A unseen grass snake slithers into the river and swims off to safety. At night deer and badgers make their way to the marshy shallows to drink, while Daubenton's bats skim over the surface like tiny hovercraft picking off the insects as they rise from the water.

Nothing could be more pleasant, but each winter, just for a few days, the river bursts its banks and floods the surrounding fields. It has been doing the same for centuries, but modern economics make no allowance for this sort of nonsense. Action is agreed; the river will be tamed. In come engineers with vast yellow machines. The first problem is that they cannot reach the bank because trees are in the way, so the trees are felled. Next, the plants in the river are said to obstruct the flow, so they are ripped out by great steel buckets. Because water tries to flow in straight lines, meanders hinder its progress, so new straight channels are dug, the old bends dry out and are filled in. Finally, to make future management easier the whole channel is cut to a symmetrical, steep sided ditch, and to make it nice and tidy the bank top smoothed into a curve by the back of an excavator bucket. When the machines go, the wildlife has gone. Only plants like nettles, which thrive on nutrient rich, disturbed ground will come back.

The damage was not only to wild plants and creatures. In some places upland rivers kicked back by undermining their new banks to change course and cause further flooding. The engineers had not noticed that trees, shrubs and masses of ground plants stabilise river banks.

This scenario was acted out dozens of times across the Midlands twenty years ago. The legacy can be seen in dull, straight rivers which are mere ditches across vast open fields. Fortunately, the protests of conservationists and ordinary people put a stop to this approach before all river habitat had been destroyed. In the 1980s, the County Wildlife Trusts began walking the river banks with the engineers in advance of work, identifying the features which should be left. The machinery drivers were given incentives to carry out works which improved the habitat for wildlife, or at least replaced what was destroyed. It was found that the machines could after all get between trees and that by working from one bank, the vegetation on the other side could be left intact. The apparently clumsy buckets on the long arms of the Hymacs could be surprisingly gentle. Tiny shallow bays could be dug from which animals could drink. Even water plants could be gently transplanted.

Today there is more sensitivity to the environment. Flood prevention works are still carried out, but usually without the mass destruction of wildlife. A good many riverbanks once cleared of trees are being replanted to prevent erosion. In places the National Rivers Authority is even building artificial otter holts to encourage these delightful animals back to the region's waterways.

Currently the NRA has 27 miles of hard flood walls in concrete, steel or brick and 495 miles of earth banks. Yearly they remove 1 million tonnes of silt, 30,000 fallen or unsafe trees and plant 250,000 trees and shrubs. They also (for some reason) mow 24 million square metres of floodbanks. Why not let them rip, improve the scale and diversity of the habitat and increase the stability of the banks?

Ominously, the NRA have a ten year schedule of new work involving some twenty contracts a year. Schemes include continuing work on the River Severn between Gloucester and Avonmouth, flood alleviation near Shrewsbury and Kidderminster to protect about four hundred properties in each place, and work at Bewdley and Upton on Severn to protect some 350 houses. There is also six years of work on the River Soar in Leicestershire between Quorn and the Trent.

NRA offer assurances that all schemes are subject to feasibility studies to ensure that the benefits from flood defence works will exceed the construction costs. They also consult local people and conservation bodies and carry out work with "particular regard" for fisheries, conservation and recreation.

Grain barges on the Severn at Tewkesbury

Navigation & transport

In several parts of Britain the remains of prehistoric boats have been dug from rivers, including two canoes of about 1000 BC from the Trent at Nottingham. Two thousand years ago the Romans built a canal across Romney Marsh in Kent and the Fosse Dyke to link the Trent to Lincoln and the River Witham and the Wash. As our modern economy developed from about 1600, coastal shipping and rivers were a vital method of transport.

The River Trent has been an important highway from the Midlands to the Humber since the Bronze Age. Old maps show it as navigable to Nottingham in 1607 and to Burton on Trent in 1724. We do not know what size of craft were involved but they were probably small.

An Act of Parliament to improve navigation was passed in 1699 and another in 1783. They led to construction of a tow path and plans for dredging, locks and weirs. Progress was patchy and the whole scheme was not completed until 1926. The Trent is now navigable to craft up to 24.69 metres long, 3.2 metres beam, .91 metres draught and 2.5 metres height (above water level) downstream from Derwent Mouth, where small craft can join the Trent & Mersey Canal. Downstream of Nottingham it is open to craft up to 44.2 metres long, 5.49 metres beam, 1.83 metres draught and 3.81 metres high.

The Severn has long been a transport artery, and no less than twelve canals are connected with the river and its estuary. In the reign of Henry VII it had been a navigation since *"time out of mind"*. The Romans built a quay at Gloucester, and a charter of Henry II in the mid 12th century said

> *"the men of Gloucester and all those who wish to go by the River Severn shall have their way and passage by the Severn with wood, coals, timber and all their merchandise freely and quietly, and we forbid anyone from vexing or disturbing them in aught hereupon".*

Worcester, Bewdley, Bridgnorth and Shrewsbury developed into inland ports. Except for Bewdley, these towns were marked on Gough's map of 1360. Home produced goods went downriver, back came wine, soap, iron, lead, oil, liquorice, oranges, alum, canvas, and linen. By the 17th century industrialisation saw scythes, nails, paper and brass pots travelling from Severnside towns.

Time was less important than cost, and water transport cost only one tenth as much as carriage by road. Early Acts of Parliament legislated for an entirely free river, but riverside towns eventually won the battle to charge tolls for goods landed on their quays. Attempts to board craft and force boatmen to sell their cargoes, or charge them for passing the towns were abandoned by the end of the 16th century.

The Severn seems to have been navigable, probably only by light craft in the upper reaches, to Shrewsbury in 1635 and Welshpool in 1727. North of Worcester was always difficult, with frequent shoals and many mills drawing off water. From the Tudor and Elizabethan times cargos grew and so did the boats, so that by the 18th century Bewdley was for many of them the limit of navigation.

Downstream, sandbanks and shoals at Gloucester were inhibiting trade on the whole river. The Staffordshire & Worcestershire Canal opened in 1772, joining the Severn at Stourport, and the Worcester & Birmingham Canal to Worcester opened in 1815. They stimulated improvements, dredging and building of the Gloucester & Sharpness Canal to carry ships into the estuary. The river south of Stourport became the navigable portion and had a regular steam tug service from the early date of 1814.

The Severn can now accommodate vessels of 27.1 metres length, 5.5 metres beam, 1.82 metres draught and 6 metres height from Stourport down to Worcester. Below Worcester dimensions can increase to 41 metres long, 6.7 metres beam, 2.4 metres draught and 7.5 metres height.

The River Avon was made navigable at colossal expense. One map shows navigation to within four miles of Warwick by 1641. Another has navigation to Stratford before 1600, but the mapmakers probably had in mind different sizes of craft. Stratford was certainly open to craft capable of carrying some sort of load by the late 1600's. Unlike the other two rivers, the Avon suffered a long period of deterioration and was almost unnavigable by the 1940's. It was bought by the Inland Waterways Association and is now controlled by the Lower and and Upper Avon Navigation Trusts. The battle to reclaim the river and other inland waterways is a breathless story and we recommend *Race Against Time* by David Bolton, Methuen ISBN 0 413 634701.

The biggest craft which can navigate the River Avon are about 23 metres long by 4 metres beam.

On all three waterways and the linked canals there is a large leisure traffic of cruisers and narrowboats. Commercial cargo traffic is limited. The Trent carries between 250,000 and 300,000 tonnes of sand and gravel annually south of Cromwell Lock, near Newark. There is no cargo traffic on the Avon, whilst on the Severn grain barges travel between Tewksbury and Sharpness.

There seem to be opportunities to make greater use of our transport resources, but there are two areas of debate. Firstly whether water transport is feasible and relevant to our need to shift goods, and possible detriment to the rivers by increased and different traffic.

Potentially barges should be able to make a contribution to our transport needs given that one 300 tonne capacity barge can replace about ten lorries. Replacing ten engines and crew with one is likely to make moving goods cheaper, and especially if road transport is properly costed to include noise, vibrations, road maintenance, traffic congestion, fumes, CO_2 emissions, and accidents. The economics of each mode of transport are not beyond human control. With grants, tax increases or rebates governments can make desired practices more attractive than alternatives.

Clearly barges cannot make deliveries to individual shops or factories unless they are on the waterside, though a canal beside each road is an enticing fantasy. Water transport is suited to bulk cargos regularly travelling long distances where speed is not critical. Suitable cargos include sand, gravel, coal, coke, fuel oils, wastes, grains, chemicals, root crops, timber, ores, cement and scrap metal. Roads are more suitable for short, local transits of lighter and high value goods, or where speed is critical.

Water transport has to be able to carry goods to where they are needed. The economics governing the size of craft which we discuss below rule out the narrow canals as links, so we are left with the rivers. The Trent has good connections to a large hinterland and the sea. The Severn has connection into Warwickshire via the Avon, and via Gloucester & Sharpness Canal to the Bristol Channel. The River Avon is linked to the Severn and the sea.

To expand water carriage there would have to be quantities of suitable cargos (as above) at waterside points. Availability would mirror the water connections. One may doubt that much would be available on the River Avon with only Stratford upon Avon and Evesham as likely ports, though there could be agricultural cargos. On the Severn the likely sources of the right type of cargos seem

to be Kidderminster, Worcester, Tewksbury and Gloucester.
We could imagine that if barge services were available and had
become significantly more attractive than road transport, some
traders might locate a works or wharf to take advantage of them.

What might all this do to the rivers and their existing traffic? Most
of the pleasure craft on the rivers are canal narrowboats of maximum
dimensions of about 23 metres length and 2 metres beam. Most
narrowboats are shorter - perhaps a popular family size would be
around 18 metres length. All three rivers also carry river cruisers
which are typically wider and shorter.

Formerly a self propelled barge of 100 tonnes capacity was economical. Compare this with the uneconomically small 20/30 tonne
capacity of narrowboats. Probably the minimum viable size now is
250/300 tonnes. This would mean craft measuring not less than, for
example 28 metres length, 6 metres beam and drawing 2.5 metres of
water. Obviously, for a greater length a craft could be of narrower
beam and draw less water. For comparison this sample barge would
be some 6 metres longer than the longest narrowboat, about 4 metres
wider and demanding nearly three times the depth of water.

The "economic barge" can be compared with maximum dimensions
for craft on the Trent and Severn;

| | (metres) | | | |
	length	beam	draught	height
Economic Barge	**28.00**	**6.00**	**2.50**	-
Trent (from Nottingham)	44.20	5.49	1.83	3.81
Severn (from Worcester)	41.00	6.70	2.40	7.50
.. (from Stourport)	27.10	5.50	1.82	6.00

The River Avon must be ruled out as a goods carrying waterway. It
could not accommodate boats of economical beam or length and height
is restricted. The Severn could cope with large enough craft up to
Worcester. Upstream there would have to be some reduction in size,
though this should not take them below viable capacity.

Additional traffic would certainly involve rather larger craft than
the majority on the rivers, which are narrow boats and small
cruisers. But its volume seems likely to be modest and unlikely to
cause more damage to the river and its environment than existing
traffic. Geography, the economics of transport, the damage done
by lorries and a new political climate, lead us to think that more
commercial traffic might be developed on the Trent and Severn.

Power generation

The Romans introduced water mills to Britain so that by the time of the Domesday Book survey there were at least 5624. We can still locate all but one hundred of the sites. The means to grind grain was vital, every village needed it, and mills were built on quite small rivers.

The Dowles Brook which joins the River Severn north of Bewdley is no torrent. Even so, there were four mills within three miles of the Severn. The River Arrow is rather bigger, and in its twelve miles from Redditch to the Avon there were eight mills, and later a forge.

In some places, where mills stood by fast flowing streams, there would have been little need for additional engineering. Elsewhere, some of the first human alterations to and streams were the building of mill races and mill ponds. These small, early works did not destroy the character of rivers but added another feature. White water crashing from a mill race would increase oxygen levels in lowland rivers to the benefit of wildlife downstream.

Water power could still be used to drive plant mechanically but we have not heard of it being done, apart from non-commercial mill restorations.

Water is now used to drive turbines and generate electricity, but this is restricted to big schemes for which larger and more powerful flows of water are required than our Midland rivers offer. However before grid electricity was connected to every remote cottage and farm, small turbines were quite common and there may still be a few in upland areas. People are again getting used to the idea that we can generate energy in small packets. Solar panels may not eliminate the need for mains electricity, but they can reduce the bills. Farms and houses near suitable rivers and streams may before long be equipped with small turbines.

Midland rivers are now involved more indirectly in power generation in that the Trent supplies cooling water to several power stations. This is, of course, returned to the river at somewhat higher temperatures, which has environmental implications. It also seems rather odd to spend all that money heating water to make steam, then after it has driven turbines, we throw the very large amount of surplus heat away into the air and the river.

Water supply

Rivers provided the power to process crops and turn them into food; they were also the lifeblood of the crops themselves. Many farms in the Midlands stood close to rivers to take advantage of the free draining soils and rich, fertile silts left by floods. In the past farmers channelled winter flows onto water meadows which were used for summer grazing, and by this means given a good start early in the season. They also diverted some river water over their fields in cold periods early in the year because shallow, slow moving water protected the grass from frosts and boosted growth. Where this still happens it is accidental rather than deliberate, something flood plain farmers make the best of.

Rivers and streams were also used to supply drinking water to the farms, towns and villages, and for industrial users such as tanners. Today there is greater pollution from some sources such as industry, much less from sewage, and we are more fastidious about what we drink. The demands are also vastly greater, and the controls (by NRA) over what may be put into and taken from rivers are essential.

Present demands are for drinking water (51%), power stations (36%), other industrial use (12%) and agriculture, including spray irrigation (1%). Supplies of 1900 Megalitres (millions of litres) per day are drawn from groundwater, reservoirs and rivers.

Water is drawn from the River Severn for Shrewsbury (at Shelton) Wolverhampton (Hampton Loade), Coventry (Strensham), Worcester (Strensham) and Gloucester (Strensham). A negligible quantity also enters Birmingham's Elan Valley water supply at Trimpley, north of Bewdley, where the famous seventy mile aqueduct crosses the Severn. The Trimpley works otherwise supplies a wide area of Worcestershire. So much abstraction for drinking water is possible because the Severn is very clean. From its source on Pumlumon it is almost unpolluted until the Stour slithers out of the Black Country to join the big river at Stourport.

There are two big dams in the Severn catchment, the Clywedog and Vyrnwy across the rivers of those names. The Clywedog Dam is part of a flow control scheme allowing some of the Severn's upland waters to be stored for release when the flow is low. It is now also used to release enough water to make sure the Severn can supply all the towns mentioned. The Vyrnwy is Liverpool's reservoir but it can sometimes augment water supplies in the Severn.

The Avon is virtually useless for water supply because of effluents from Rugby and Coventry, but supplies are drawn off for local use above Rugby. Rugby and the Warwick - Leamington Spa area are supplied from the River Leam. From personal experience we can say that the water is not pleasant tasting. This is not surprising since is has run off arable farming land collecting lots of nitrates, and for other reasons has been bashed pretty hard with chlorine.

The Trent has long been unsuitable for drinking water, although its tributaries the Blythe, Dove and Derwent are all used. We talk about pollution below. Trent water is used in the various power stations ranged beside it and many other industrial uses. But NRA report that improved water treatment methods are causing several water supply companies to think of taking supplies at points between its Staffordshire source and Lincolnshire.

Demand for water is affected by population growth, leakage from supply systems, evaporation, industrial activity, gardening and the weather, and quite markedly by domestic metering. Supply is also affected by the weather, and by increased industrial pollution, more nitrates, leakage, the extent to which, for example, farmers can store water in ponds in winter for summer irrigation, and the possibility of transfering water between areas. The NRA's strategy is to try to manage demand and maximise available supplies through some of these factors which are within their control, before resorting to major investment in dams and reservoirs.

Rivers for play; recreation

Leisure pursuits may be play for the public but to the rivers they are work. Leisure is serious business in Britain and one of the most expanding areas of the economy. Governments obviously think leisure and the arts are sufficiently important to society to have Ministers, even if they don't give them much money to spend.

The waterways system has an enormous capacity to provide leisure. It is as much an assett as swimming pools, parks and tennis courts. And like our network of public footpaths, but unlike most other such assetts, waterways can absorb millions of people at the same time at virtually no extra cost per head. Rivers support three main recreations, angling, boating and walking. Walking is rather incidental to rivers, as river banks are to walking, because they are only likely to form part of any walk and there are alternatives.

Angling is one of Britain's most popular leisure activities, probably not far behind TV and sex. Annually some 250,000 licences are sold in the Severn Trent region.

The River Severn and its tributaries the Dene, Frome, Leadon, Teme, Clun, Onny, Corve, Rea, Tern, Roden, Perry, Meese and various others outside the area of this book, support almost every type of freshwater fish. The Avon is also first class, with its tributaries the Arrow, Alne, Stour and Leam.

In these rivers a good angler might catch barbel, chubb, bream, roach, perch, dace, pike, gudgeon, rudd and the dreaded zander, an east European alien predator that is spreading steadily. Over 3,000 salmon are caught each year on the Severn south of Gloucester, and about 1,000 in the rest of the river

The Trent has historically been and still is, one of Britain's best coarse fisheries. Huge sturgeon were caught up to 1902. Do not expect too much of its Birmingham tributary the Tame, but there is excellent fishing on the Dove and the Derwent. Pollution control on the main river in recent years has encouraged fish to increase. Some thirty five species of fish can be found, including barbel, roach, chub, dace, bream, silver bream, pike, carp and gudgeon.

Some of the NRA investment in angling is in the form of what they would do anyway, pollution control and maintaining river flow. In addition they provide fish passes at weirs and measures mentioned as part of the general conservation effort. At Calverton near Nottingham NRA have one of the biggest fish farms in Europe, from which they restock rivers as necessary and sell to owners of lakes and ponds.

Boating usually takes the forms of cruising and canoeing. Day boat hire, sailing and water skiing can be found at a few places. Cruising is not cheap, but any visit to the Severn, Avon or Trent will show that it is remarkably popular, even in bleak and blustery weather. Cruising is restricted by navigation limits, but canoeists can go very much further.

The public investment in boating comes through British Waterways Board's expenditure on repairing banks and towpaths, dredging and maintaining locks and bridges. Only a comparatively small part relates to river navigations. Costs are partly recovered from sale of boat licences.

If footpaths and waterways cost that emotive commodity - public money, to maintain them for recreational use, compare the amount with the cost of building, running and maintaining swimming pools or golf courses to provide for the same number of people.

Cooling towers at Rugeley

The modern bridge and busy moorings at Upton on Severn

Pollution & Conservation

The Midlands is heavily populated with more that its fair share of industry. Outside towns and cities there are still large rural areas, but most are intensively farmed. High population levels, agriculture and industry can all cause serious river pollution.

Under the National Rivers Authority's General Quality Assessment, river waters were until 1994 classified into five grades, 1A, 1B, 2, 3, and 4. Each had a detailed scientific specification. For example, Grade A quality water must contain at least 80% of the oxygen that pure water can disolve, and ammonia content must be less than .4 milligrams per litre (4 ten thousandths of a gram). Grade B must have 60% oxygen saturation and ammonia under .9mg/l. There were many other requirements for each grade.

New and more detailed criteria for assessment were adopted in 1994. River samples are to be assessed under four headings, described as "windows", in that each represents a different way of looking at rivers. Specifications have not yet been devised for them all but the "chemical content" window is in use.

* **chemical content** (disolved oxygen, biochemical oxygen demand and ammonia)

* **biological** (numbers of specified creatures with more points allocated to ones intolerant of pollution, such as mayflys and nymphs, and lower points for tolerant worms)

* **nutrient** (nitrates, phosphorus)

* **aesthetic** (colour, smell, litter).

Each section of each river is to be allocated a letter grade, A to F for each window. Since only the chemical content specification is in use, grades currently published by NRA are for this aspect. However, for our purposes this seems likely to give readers a reasonable assessment of the general health of our rivers.

We refer to current published grades as we discuss the rivers, but at this stage a few examples might clarify what they mean. Grade A water is of the highest quality. You find it in the mountainous upper reaches of the River Severn, and the River Team as it rushes off the Kerry Hills. Grade C water has probably taken run off from roads and farmland and some effluents from what used to be called Sewage Works, now more politely (and accurately) known as Water Treatment Plants. A good example is the River Arrow which runs through Redditch to the Avon, where quality varies between grades C and D. Grade E water is likely to be found in rivers running through urban and industrial areas, such as the Tame. Under the new system there is a Grade F, which must be only a step away from "run for your lives". We have only a mile of it in the Midlands at purification lakes on the River Tame, where nasties are being deliberately concentrated for removal. Presumably if such conditions occured elsewhere the NRA would take emergency action so they would be temporary.

The following table shows (with thanks to NRA) the percentage lengths of rivers in each quality class over four years:

	GOOD		FAIR		POOR	BAD
	A	B	C	D	E	F
1990	9.3	23.5	32.4	14.9	17.9	2.0
1992	6.7	31.7	28.0	16.9	13.5	3.2
1993	8.2	31.5	33.1	12.4	12.0	2.8
1994	9.1	32.7	33.3	13.8	10.2	.9

Bear in mind that like a company's balance sheet, quality grades are no more than snapshots taken at a particular time. River quality varies daily and by the season, For example the long, dry summer of 1995 drastically reduced the flow of all rivers, but effluent discharges would remain normal and reduce water quality.

The figures show movement in the right direction, but the improvements since 1990 followed five years of repeated downgradings. Here are some local examples of changed gradings between 1990 and 1993.

UPGRADINGS

	From	Kms	Grades
SEVERN			
R Teme (Mid Wales)	Beguildy	32	C to B

AVON

R Swift (Rugby)	Easenhall Brook	5	E	C
R Smite (Rugby)	Clawson Lane	6	E	D
R Arrow (Redditch)	Spernal	8	D	C

TRENT

R Penk (Cannock)	Saredon Brook	21	D	C
R Sow (Stafford)	Brancote	5	D	C
R Tame (Wolverhampton)	Stow Heath	6	F	E
R Anker (Nuneaton)	Nuneaton	7	E	D
R Dove (Burton o T)	Tutbury	10	D	C

DOWNGRADINGS

SEVERN

Mad Brook (Telford)	Madeley	7		
Mor Brook (Bridgnorth)	Muckley	12	B	D
Madresfield Brook (Malvern)	Madresfield	4	A	B
			B	D

AVON

Kingswood Brook (Solihull)	Stratford Canal 5		C	D

When describing each river we mention water quality at different points but can now offer an overview.

The Severn and its tributaries above Shrewsbury fall mostly into grade A. Given the upland catchment, lack of people and industry in mid Wales and low intensity farming, this is to be expected. By Shrewsbury the Severn has deteriorated slightly to grade B, but is still of good quality. The water in the Severn stays good for much of its length, due largely to the high standard of most of its tributaries. It adequately dilutes the Stour (Grade E) which gurgles murkily out of the Black Country to join the Severn at Stourport.

The furthest headwaters of the Avon are not currently graded but they soon become Grade B and decline to C in Rugby. The Sowe which drains Coventry brings Grade E water, reducing the Avon to Grade D. The Leam at Leamington Spa helps it recover to Grade C, which it remains for the rest of its journey to the Severn, helped by the Grade B waters of the Warwickshire Stour.

The Trent starts off as a clean upland stream but within a few miles reaches Stoke on Trent. For a tiny river such a large industrial city is a major handicap, and the water quickly deteriorates to Grade

D. At Essex Bridge near Shugborough you can see the effect of the cleaner waters of the Sow, but they cannot raise the quality above C. After collecting the rather nasty Tame north of Tamworth (Grade E) it declines to Grade D until the cleaner Dove and Derwent restore it to Grade C, and so it fluctuates down to the Humber.

New and improved water treatment works are doing a great deal to clean up our rivers and are responsible for most of the progress shown in the first table. In our area important examples are at Nuneaton (River Anker), Minworth, Birmingham (Tame), Cannock (Penk), Leek (Churnet) and Spernal near Redditch (Arrow). They are required to meet standards laid down by EU legislation which member states are obliged to reach within certain periods. The British government often claims we need more time to meet them, but environmentalists (who are not impressed) can now use the standards to apply pressure for change; moral pressure and ulitmately, legal action in the EU Court.

Some rivers have particularly intractable problems. The Tame river system has the dirty job of draining much of Birmingham and the Black Country. It is not a large river so the impact from so many people and so much industry is the greater. Star contributors are an old waste tip at Goscote, Walsall, contaminated land at Darlaston and run off from Spaghetti Junction. Through the conurbation the water quality is Grade E. It improves only after Minworth on the eastern edge of the conurbation, where a big treatment works tackles much the area's waste water.

The NRA operates purification lakes at Lea Marston about a mile downstream of the Minworth works. Taking an area of abandoned sand and gravel pits, they contructed three lakes - romantically named Lake Tame, Lake Lester and Reeve Mere. All floating debris is swept off the water and solids allowed to settle. The deposits are pumped away as sludge, and the water squeezed out of them is further cleaned before being returned to the river. Incredibly the lakes have become important winter habitat for waterbirds. There are herons and swans, tufted duck, potchard and coots. As a result of all this, the lower reaches of the Tame are nearly Grade D. Below the lakes there is now a coarse fishery where angling clubs hold competitions.

Reduction of the amount of industry in the area has cut pollution, so have improvements to sewage works. The NRA are trying to deal with the problem of land contamination with the aim of raising the quality of the Tame within the conurbation to Grade D.

Water treatment is the controlled and approved way of disposing of waste water but what it contains may still leave harmful substances in the effluent. Added to this permitted burden of our rivers, unpredictable leaks or deliberate releases can be disastrous. NRA figures for 1993 group main sources of pollution as follows: Oil 34%, Farm waste 9.9%, Suspended solids 9.6%, Chemicals 6.2%, Sewage 22.9%, Colourings 4.6% and Other 11.1%. This summary includes textile dyes, farm herbicides, slurry and fertilisers, run off from waste tips, potato processing effluent, sheep dip residues and mothproofers from carpet factories, petrol and oils from tanks and garages, salt and oils washed from roads, sewage escapes, milk thrown away by farmers to avoid quota penalties, waste water and oils from boats, and water from old mines. The last is an an increasing problem following closure of many pits, where water which was formally pumped now escapes uncontrolled.

Here are some examples of particular problems. Farm slurry and silage liquor are over 200 times more polluting than human sewage. If they get into a river they can kill all life for miles. The first evidence is usually a mass of dead floating fish. Slurry is liquid-ised cattle manure swept or hosed from yards and kept in a tank or pond until it can be spread over the land. Silage is compressed grass from which air has been excluded which is stored as winter feed. It has largely (and nastily) superceded dry storage as hay because silage can be cut wet, rather important in our climate. As the silage matures it releases a dark brown liquid. Amazingly, animals will drink it and benefit, but it can also leak away.

If these two liquids get into a watercourse they provide food for bacteria, which multiply and consume all the oxygen in the water. Both contain ammonia which is a straightforward poison. They also contain nutrients which accelerate growth of waterplants and surface algae, clogging the watercourse and making the water unfit to drink.

Oil is a serious problem, particularly when tanks stand close to the water. Apart from accidental leakage or deliberate discharge by owners, there are a thankfully small minority of lunatics who empty such tanks into rivers for fun. Oil forms a thin film over the water surface, you can imagine how far even a litre would spread. This acts rather like a plastic bag to block out oxygen. It also coats waterbirds and is directly toxic.

Oil has long been covered by regulations to prevent fire and health and safety problems, but not specifically to prevent pollution. The Control of Pollution (Silage, Slurry and Agricultural Fuel Oil)

Regulations 1991 now apply to new, enlarged or reconstructed farm storage arrangements of more then 1,500 litres capacity. However, if older ones present a significant pollution risk the NRA can insist on improvements. Farmers are required to build tanks and ponds to last 20 years, and more than 10 metres from any watercourse. Vessel capacity and construction are specified, in particular there must be safe drains to prevent escapes.

Farmers and others who cause or permit escapes which enter watercourses can be prosecuted by the NRA and incur heavy fines, whatever the age or capacity of their arrangements. However there seems no reason why precautionary regulations should apply only to farmers. In cases where the new regulations are not binding, they will form a useful code of practice which any storer of oil might apply voluntarily to avoid trouble.

Pesticides and herbicides are another source of serious pollution. They are supplied in concentrated form and designed to be diluted, bringing problems of inadequate dilution, spillage during mixing, escape while equipment is being washed out, and disposal of containers. Spraying may be uneven, creating concentrations, or falling directly into watercourses. These substances are designed as poisons. Some now act more selectively on specific unwanted plants and creatures and do not remain in the food chain, like the infamous DDT, but they can still cause great damage.

All fertilizers contain the same three essential plant foods in different proportions, nitrogen, phosphorous and potassium. They are spread in amounts per hectare recommended by manufacturers and no doubt modern spreaders do it very evenly. But excessive amounts are not being taken up by the crops because too much is washed into underground storage and rivers. These substances cause overgrowth of some water plants and algae and affect the taste and wholesomeness of drinking water. In the Midlands nitrates are the single most important pollutant of groundwater (ie - underground water, not rivers) and under an EU Directive special measures are bring taken in 36 areas in the Severn Trent catchment. One scheme specifically covers surface water in the River Leam, which supplies (not very nice) water to Rugby, Leamington Spa, Warwick and Kenilworth.

In so called Nitrate Vulnerable Zones farmers are required to limit fertilizer use, though this involves no more than complying with the Code of Good Agricultural Practice and following the fertilizer makers recommendations. We are not certain how this can be accurately and continuously monitored.

Once alerted, the National Rivers Authority do what they can to contain pollution. They can set up booms to hold back surface slicks, pump out polluted areas and rescue oiled birds. They also set about finding and prosecuting culprits, but tracing the source of pollution in a river or stream which may have travelled a distance can be difficult and time consuming.

When researching for this book John Roberts went to the River Tame at Hopwas near Tamworth. The whole width of the river was covered in rainbows of oil, so he used a phone box at the end of the bridge to phone the NRA. After some work downstream he drove to Tamworth and traced the river, to find that the pollution must have started at a small industrial estate within a few hundred yards of Hopwas bridge. The NRA inspector later said that he had visited the scene within fifteen minutes of the alert and come to the same conclusion. However, inspection of the outfalls had shown no trace of oil so no one could be warned or prosecuted. We must say through, that the NRA's response was very impressive.

If you see any evidence of water pollution in rivers and streams, phone the NRA immediately on their emergency line - 0800 80 70 60. They will send you a free plastic card for your wallet, calls are free and lines open 24 hours a day.

Make sure you do not cause pollution. It is an offence to pour any waste product directly into waterways or to use rivers as dumps, even for garden rubbish. Do not pour waste oil down the drain. Take it to a collecting point for proper disposal; your local council should be able to direct you to the nearest one. How do your drains run? Make sure that kitchen and bathroom waste water joins the foul sewer and not the surface water drain, which may carry run off from your gutters straight into streams.

Monitoring water levels on the Avon near Lilbourne

Wildlife of Rivers & Streams

We cannot offer you a guide to recognition of all the wild plants and creatures mentioned in this book. It would have taken up far too much space and there are plenty of excellent books available; several appear in the Reading List.

If you have experience of watching wildlife you will know what sort of reference books you like. Beginners may find that to start with chunky manuals detailing all the wild flowers or butterflies of Eurasia is confusing. However a very useful book is Collins Field Guide to Freshwater Life by R Fitter and R Manuel. Alternatively you will need separate books for trees, flowers, butterflies, birds, fungi and insects.

Compared with its predecessor in this QuercuS series, *Midlands Woods & Forests,* there is less about wildlife and more about the history and present state of the rivers. This is because whilst there are obvious differences between various stretches of river, their wildlife is rather more uniform than in different woods.

Otter resting

River wildlife will change with soil and management, but many of our riversides are intensively farmed, leaving few natural stretches along the banks. So although one mile will differ from another, the general range of species will be fairly uniform over long distances. Rather than repeat this information we have drawn it together in this section. In the accounts of each main river we have highlighted special features. This generally means that the wildlife of riverside nature reserves gets a special mention because it's different. There is still plenty to discover along other reaches if you look.

Freshwater can support an amazing variety of wildlife, from microscopic plants and animals to large birds and mammals, like herons and otters. Rivers and streams have their own specialised species, adapted to withstand being swept away by the current.

The current is an important part of life in this wet world. Ponds and lakes do not have a current, even if they have inlets and outlets. Neither do canals. They look like rivers but the water does not flow, it moves when a lock gate is opened.

Speed of flow depends on how far downstream you are. Most rivers start in uplands as tiny, fast flowing streams which tumble quickly downhill. As they go on they combine with others to form broader, deeper brooks. Usually finding the most direct way downhill, they soon reach flatter ground, their speed of flow reduces and the river becomes more mature. By the time they have reached much of the Midlands they will have become broad and meandering like the Trent or Lower Severn.

There are some young, fast flowing streams in the region. Down the Ashes Valley on Long Mynd a stream tumbles over boulders through bleak moorland. It does not flow straight, but dodges round rock outcrops as it cuts its V shaped valley between bracken and heather covered slopes. Just outside the area of this book the River Trent starts as a tiny, oxygen rich stream on the edge of Biddulph Moor in the Pennine foothills.

Plants

Plants which live in, rather than alongside rivers and streams have to take special precautions not to get washed away. In many rivers you will find a totally submerged plant, water milfoil. This has masses of finely divided leaves which offer little resistance to the current. So long as they are firmly anchored to the river bed and do not become too big, they simply wave around in the water. Their stems are designed to break easily, so during a flood a few shoots may be lost but the plant will stay put.

Many water plants have several different shaped leaves on the same plant. Broad leaved pondweed has thread like leaves beneath the surface, but also sprouts broad floating leaves, which are helped by a bend in the stalk just below the surface. They offer a bigger surface area for photosynthesis than the narrow leaves, and a base from which the flowering stalk can project into the air.

Pollination is a problem for water plants since pollen is easily damaged by water. Water crowfoot grows in some of our slow flowing, shallow streams, poking its attractive white flowers above the surface where they can be pollinated by passing insects in the usual way. Water starwort has become truly aquatic by producing pollen containing water resistant oil. There is a single stamen on male flowers near the surface. The female flowers are lower down the stem and the pollen drifts down onto the long female styles to fertilise them.

Many smaller streams are fringed by a rich band of vegetation, which may include watercress, fool's watercress, brooklime and water forget me not.

Watercress is a member of the cabbage family and widespread in small streams. Its tiny white flowers are only 6mm across and can be found from May to October. You are advised not to take any home for salad from Midland rivers - see the section on *Pollution* etc.

The leaves of fool's watercress give it a superficial resemblance to true watercress, but the difference should become obvious when the flowers open. Fool's watercress is an umbellifer, so is related to plants like cow parsley and carrot. It is not poisonous, but not too good to eat.

Brooklime is one of the speedwells, those attractive blue flowered plants which are common in fields and lawns. It has fleshy, blunt oval leaves and is widespread, flowering from May to September.

Water forget me not is one of a great host of forget me nots which all look fairly similar. There are differences between them and this one, not surprisingly, grows only in wet places. An attractive sight, especially where it grows en masse.

Along the edges of many streams there will be muddy margins, which are exposed from time to time. This is the place to look for marsh marigold, a showy relative of the buttercups flowering in spring and early summer.

There are many places in the region where the summer river bank will be brightened by the colourful flowers of purple loosestrife. Where it grows it can be abundant and is usually very attractive to insects. Conservationists regard it as an asset, unlike the very invasive Himalayan balsam.

This plant, which is also called policeman's helmet, is tall and showy with pink and white flowers. It often grows 2 metres high and has a richly flowery scent which can become rather sickly. Introduced from India, it has spread along most waterways to the detriment of other plants. This illustrates the problems caused by introduced (or alien) species. In Canada and the United States where purple loosestrife has been introduced they have a similar problem. In Minnesota loosestrife seeds are estimated to occur at the rate of 410,000 per square metre. The plant's distribution is mapped by remote sensing from satellite so that its spread can be controlled by spraying.

Aliens tend to do one of two things in their new home. Either they cannot digest the local food supply and/or have no defence to the native diseases and predators, in which case they simply perish. Alternatively, they have no native predators, stay in rude health and manage very well. The newcomers have developed outside their new environment so they have no niche, and usually offer neither bed nor board to the local bugs.

Another alien balsam on Midland river banks is the orange balsam. This is much smaller than Himalayan balsam and does not spread so rapidly, so is less of a problem. However, a glance through old records shows that it is spreading at a steady rate.

Another showy plant of the water margins is yellow flag, its large yellow flowers out from May to July. After the flowers the great, bulky seed pods develop. These are three angled capsules which allow the brown seeds to be carried on the water to new sites. The chances of a seedling growing to maturity through the water are quite slim, so the plants also spread by thick, underground rhizomes.

You will find the piratical and familiar rosebay willowherb and related species on the river bank, but most characteristic of this

habitat is great hairy willowherb. Growing up to 1.5 metres tall
it has a mass of bright pink flowers with white centres. It is
also known as codlings and cream, from the red, codling apples.

Meadowsweet is an unusual plant. Find leaves early in the season
and they will seem very coarse. The stems and leaves are tough,
like those of a tree, but when meadowsweet is in bloom the massed
heads of creamy white flowers dissolve in a delicate haze. It is
always buzzing with eager insects reaching for nectar. Its relative,
water avens, is much less conspicuous and much less widespread
in the region, preferring limestone soils.

Wooded river banks, especially on lime rich soils, may be carpeted
by ramsons, or wild garlic. The broad, shiny green leaves appear
early in the spring and are most obvious if you walk through them.
Trampling releases the garlic like aroma which you will either love
or hate. The carpet of starry white flowers starts to appear in
April and may last well into June.

Trees

Most species of tree grow by rivers and streams but the most
widespread and typical are probably alders and the various willows.

Alder likes wet places, often growing with its roots in the water.
It is a deciduous tree with tough leaves which turn dull green in
summer. They are shaped rather like hazel, but well rounded at the
ends, taper down towards the stalk and are often completely covered
with tiny pimples. These are galls or swellings caused by mites which
live inside. The short, round female catkins resemble small fir cones
which hang on the tree all winter. Alder is often coppiced (cut down
to the stump) and allowed to regrow. The timber is a distinctive
orange red and was used to make tools and clogs.

Willows present enormous problems to people trying to identify them.
There are many types which often hybridise to produce plants which
have features of more than one species. Most obvious in spring are
the sallow and goat willow which both produce conspicuous catkins in
March and April. In some places you will also see aspen, a species of
poplar with light grey bark marked rather like a silver birch. The
leaf stalk is very long and slightly flattened, causing the leaves
to tremble in the wind.

Willow by the Severn just downstream of Bewdley

Alders by the Avon near Bubbenhall church. The cluster of trunks suggests past coppicing which was abandoned.

A tree which should be more common since it is a native of the Midlands is the black poplar. Growing in wet places and beside rivers and streams, they have heavily ridged brown bark and the trunk often bears masses of protruding bosses. The crown is rather random and untidy and the diamond shaped or oval leaves bright green and glossy. Black poplars do not grow from suckers but depend on successful seed. For this reason and because other poplars produce better timber they have not been much planted and are becoming scarce. The Wildlife Trusts are trying to promote a recovery.

Spineless wonders

Invertebrates are animals without backbones which make up a large proportion of the creatures living in rivers and streams. Like the plants, they are affected by the current, so are designed to resist or be able to swim against it.

If you cannot easily swim against the current, you are better off near the bottom. Measurements show that the fastest moving water is in the centre of the stream close to the surface. As you go deeper the current slows and there is a very thin layer, just over the bottom and only a millimetre or so thick, where there is virtually no current. Some invertebrates are adapted to exploit this miniscule layer.

Mayflies are most noticed when they leave the water on a warm evening to live out their short adult lives, during which they mate and lay eggs. They will live just a few days. Depending on the species they will have spent between a couple of months to the previous two years in the water as larvae. They have broad, flattened heads and rest on stones facing the current so their heads offer least resistance to the water. The modification of the first pair of gills to form suckers helps them to hold their position in the strongest current.

The larvae of black flies, not the aphids on your dahlias but the thingies that bite you on warm nights by the water, can fix themselves to stones in three ways. This is just as well given that they live on stones in the fastest parts of the stream.

Caddis flies do not seem to make much effort to stop themselves being washed away. They live on the tops and sides of stones in a bulky case made of debris and small pebbles. It projects well into the faster flowing water, so they have to cling on with their strong claws. The reason for such an apparently unsuitable home is that the density of the case helps hold it fast. Caddis larvae living in faster flowing water build their cases of heavier pebbles. Where the current is slower they use bits of vegetation and sand grains.

It may seem more sensible to live under than on top of stones. Many animals do, but in some rivers the current here can be so slow that it brings them almost no oxygen. They therefore choose places where they can lodge fast, but where the gentle flow of water keeps a steady temperature and brings a steady supply of oxygen.

The most typical animal of this niche is the 25mm long freshwater shrimp. Although flattened from side to side they are not very streamlined, so need to hide beneath stones to hold their position. They can cling to the bottom and even swim upright in the water, though not against the current. During the day at least ninety per cent of shrimps crawl under stones, but they do not stay there at night. With many other small invertebrates they become active between sunset and sunrise, and may drift some way in the current. They are an important source of food to fish, many of which start moving at the same times.

Like many freshwater invertebrates, dragonflies spend most of their lives as larvae or nymphs beneath the water. Once they take flight they are one of our most spectacular insects. Their habit of regularly patrolling a territory and large size earn them the name of the "bird watcher's insect", as they can be watched through binoculars. Damselflies are equally well known and can be as colourful.

The large red and blue tailed damselflies are widespread, with the blue tailed common on slow moving streams. The common blue damselfly prefers still waters like ponds and lakes, although it can be found along some very slow rivers like the Anker, near Tamworth. The banded agrion is one of the largest damselflies so is often confused with the dragonflies. It is a particularly striking insect with bright blue bands across its otherwise transparent wings. Clear, shallow silty streams, particularly in upland areas, are the places to spot the gold ringed dragonfly.

Fish

If you are an angler you do not need to be told that fish are interesting. Yet for most people including many naturalists, they are not. This may have a lot to do with the difficulties non anglers face in watching them.

Some clear streams present few problems. You can stand on a bridge and watch the fish swimming below in brown pools. Make sure that the shadow of the bridge falls across the water so that glare from the sky is not reflected from the surface. Alternatively, or as well, wear Polaroid sunglasses. Do not let your shadow fall onto the water because the fish will rush for cover, your strange moving shadow could be a predator.

As predators themselves, fish depend on a healthy population of smaller animals. If these are affected by pollution, so are the fish. Different species of fish feed on different creatures, so their presence or absence will affect what fish you can see.

From the bank, the sorts of fish which you are likely to see coming to the river surface to take flies are trout, dace, bleak, chub and roach. They all occur in Midland rivers although the trout depends on well oxygenated, clean water. In fact there are two species of trout, the brown trout, which is native, and the introduced rainbow trout. Both are members of the group of fish which includes the salmon. Trout tend to live in smaller waters, hence the terms trout stream and salmon river. Trout are more widespread than people may think but distribution is patchy. In some places they have vanished following past pollution and not returned because part of the river is still not clean enough. In others they have been reintroduced.

Salmon are often used to indicate the state of a river. In the nineteenth century even rivers like the Trent were major salmon fisheries. However, the salmon suffers from industry, and from weirs and dams which hinder passage upstream. In recent years a small number of salmon have gone as far upstream as Castle Donington, Leicestershire, and there are suggestions of a reintroduction programme.

Dace are slim, silvery fish which average about 350mm (12ins) long. They feed on invertebrates and vegetable matter and form shoals near the surface of fast running water. They spawn early in the year in gravelly reaches and usually mature in the first year.

On the Avon by the old bridge, Pershore

Gipsywort

Another slim, silvery fish is the bleak which usually grows to about 250mm (8ins). It does not breed until well into the spring and can take up to three years to mature.

Roach prefer slower rivers where they usually shoal near weed beds to feed on plants and invertebrates. Each female lays between 5000 and 200,000 eggs, though many will not hatch and most of the others will not mature. If the habitat becomes overcrowded the fish may be stunted.

Chub can be seen shoaling in rivers where they feed on invertebrates, but larger ones tend to be more or less solitary. They then defend individual territories to protect their food supply which may include plants and some smaller fish.

In the smaller streams you are most likely to spot trout, minnow and dace feeding at the surface. Out of sight, on the bottom, lampreys may be attached to stones, whilst stone loach and miller's thumb hide under the stones. Many waters will support grayling, stickleback and that ferocious predator, the pike.

Birds

River and stream side birds include many of those which occur generally throughout the countryside. Most will have no direct connection with the waterway but there are some more intimately linked with flowing water, perhaps because they eat fish or other water creatures.

The most colourful is the kingfisher. No other British bird can match its blue and orange. People are often surprised just how widespread kingfishers are. A 1993 survey by the Wildlife Trusts and Severn Trent found them along most rivers in the region, although they were nowhere common. This is because they defend their territory from all other kingfishers, including their own offspring, to secure a supply of small fish. They are also limited by their need for vertical earth banks in which to dig nesting tunnels. Even so, there are few stretches of river where you stand no chance of seeing the electric blue flash or hearing the high pitched whistle of a kingfisher.

Another widespread fish eater is the heron. You cannot miss these big grey birds in flight, but standing quiet and stick like in the shallows, dagger beak waiting for a fish, they may be almost invisible. They nest in trees which might be by the river, a small lake or even in woods.

On some upland waters in the region, dippers are quite common. Shaped like overgrown, white breasted wrens, you may see them bobbing up and down on a boulder in the centre of a fast flowing river. Now and then they will walk into the water, "flying" under the surface after invertebrates. They have more chance of finding food in the streams of limestone country because these support the most insect life. Dippers are found on more acid streams, but as they become yet more acid from air pollution they support less insect life.

Wagtails are typical waterside birds. The pied wagtail will nest in a host of places away from water and many never venture near it. But its relatives the yellow and grey wagtails are more tied to water.

The yellow wagtail is a summer visitor and the one most likely to be seen along lowland rivers. It nests on the ground, often in the shelter of a plant. It is a bright yellow bird with olive green upper parts. Grey wagtails are yellow below, but have a grey back. You will find them along upland streams, in the same sort of places as dippers. Like dippers they feed on invertebrates and often nest in a hole under a bridge.

The marsh warbler is a Midlands speciality. Like most warblers, it is small, greenish, and most easily distinguished by its voice. In the case of the marsh warbler this is a combination of up to seventy imitations of other British and African bird songs in half an hour. Marsh warblers are widespread in Europe and they like dense willowherbs, meadowsweet, nettles and the like, so you would expect them to be common here. In fact, there have only been a few dozen pairs in Britain, which may have something to do with our island isolation. Some other common European birds like golden orioles are similarly restricted. The most consistent breeding areas have been the Severn and Avon valleys in Worcestershire, but even here there has been a decline. The 1992 West Midland Bird Club report says: "By early June four males were there (in the Avon Valley), but with only one female, breeding success was limited to a single pair". A girl can only do so much.

You will meet many familiar water birds along rivers and streams, - mallard, coot, moorhen and little grebe. Look out for the occasional water rail, a bird closely related to the moorhen, but far more secretive. These spend much of their time skulking in vegetation along muddy margins, sometimes giving out a pig like squeal.

Mammals

As with birds, many mammals come to rivers and streams to drink. Here, we confine ourselves to those which depend on water.

Among the small mammals is the water shrew, by far the most distinctive shrew, with contrasting dark upper and pale lower sides. Although usually found near streams and ponds, where it can swim well, it may turn up several kilometres from the water. It is common where it occurs, but distribution in the region is scattered with a bias towards the north.

Of the bats, one of the most easily identified near water is Daubenton's. Like the water shrew, they have contrasting dark upper and pale lower parts, but their give away feature is hunting for insects by flying low over the water like little hovercraft. Records suggest they are very thinly distributed, but this may reflect lack of effort in looking. Once a determined effort has been made to find them, they have turned up at a number of Midland waters where they had not been recorded.

Water voles are often called water rats, but are not related to rats. They are by far the largest voles and you may seen them sitting on their hind legs chewing at a piece of vegetation held in their two front paws. Water voles are widespread throughout the region, though recent studies have suggested a decline. Some people associate this with the spread of mink.

Mink were introduced from North America in the 1930s to stock fur farms. Some escaped and others were deliberately released. Mink have spread through much of the country and are now blamed, amongst other things, for indiscriminately killing birds. Experience at some sites suggests that this is true, but other research has not ident- ified any link. There is much prejudice, so until definitive research proves one way or the other, the case remains open. Mink are often confused with otters, but are much smaller and darker.

The Midland otter population is expanding, especially eastwards through Shropshire and into Worcestershire and Staffordshire.

Further east there is less chance of otters being present, but the situation is changing all the time. Otters were once more common but declined from the 1950s, largely due to a build up of persistent organochlorine pesticides in their prime food, fish. Restrictions on the use of DDT and other chemicals has allowed the recovery.

The plants and creatures we have described are only a few of those which you might find on Midland rivers and streams. If you want to learn more, join your county Wildlife Trust (see advert at the front). They all hold regular walks, talks and splashy events.

Purple Loosetrife

River Severn

The River Severn starts life as a remote pool high on the slopes of Pumlumon between Aberystwyth and Llanidloes. The source is near the county boundary between Dyfed and Powys, about 12 miles from the sea and close to the springs of two other rivers.

In 1854 George Borrow took his famous walk through Wales which he recounted in *Wild Wales*. At Devil's Bridge he engaged a guide who lead him to the summit of Pumlumon to visit the sources of the Severn, Wye and Rheidol.

"A mountainous wilderness extended on every side, a waste of russet coloured hills, with here and there a black, craggy summit. No signs of life or cultivation were to be discovered, and the eye might search in vain for a grove or even a single tree."

Borrow was not satisfied with just looking at the source of the Rheidol from the edge of a *"very craggy and precipitous place"*. Against the advice of his guide, they climbed hairaisingly down to the lake so that Borrow could drink from the source. He explains - *"in order that … I may … be able to harangue about them in a tone of confidence and authority."*

"The source of the Rheidol is a small, beautiful lake, about a quarter of a mile in length. It is overhung on the east and north by frightful crags, from which it is fed by a number of small rills. The water is of the deepest blue and of very considerable depth."

Next they went to see the "ffynon" (spring or well) of the Severn, which the guide kept explaining was *"higher up the nant"*(stream).

"The source of the Severn is a little pool of water some twenty inches long, six wide and about three deep. It is covered at the bottom with small stones, from between which the water gushes up. It is on the left hand side of the nant as you ascend, close to the very top."

After Borrow had drunk from the pool, the guide lead him - *"within fifteen minutes to the source of the Wye."*

".... which is a little pool … near the top of a grassy hill which forms part of the Great Pumlumon. The stream, after leaving its

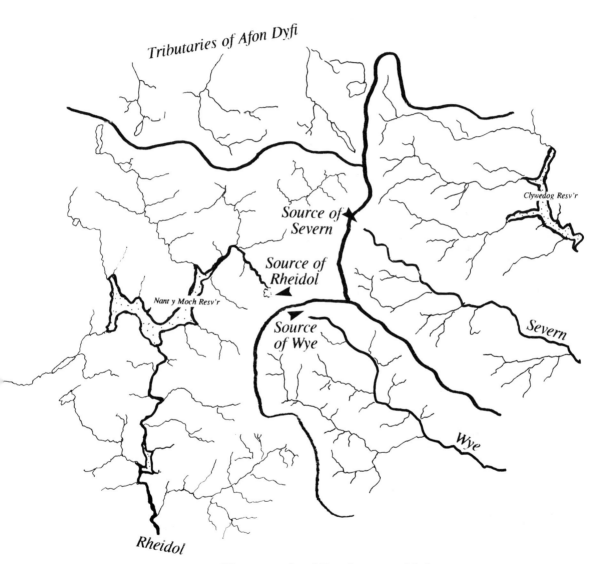

The summit of Pumlumon with heavy
lines showing the watersheds.

source, runs down the hill towards the east ... The fountains of the
Severn and Wye are in close proximity to each other. That of the
Rheidol stands somewhat apart from both, as if, proud of its own
beauty, it disdained the other two for their homliness. All three
are contained within the compass of a mile."

Take no notice of Borrow's geography and distances, which are
as romantically fanciful as his Welsh and many of his stories. We
show the sources on the sketch map. However, during his visit the
guide refers to the river as "Afon Hafren", the English name is
a close copy, and "haf" is the Welsh for summertime.

The sources may be near the coast, but the Severn flows in the
opposite direction. Britain's longest river takes about 180 miles
to complete its journey to the Bristol Channel. The River Wye also
heads inland, but on a more direct, south-easterly route, and finally
joins the Severn beneath the Severn Road Bridge, near Chepstow in
the estuary. The source of the Rheidol is a little further west, and
it crashes down through Devil's Bridge and its deep, steep and
beautiful valley to meet the sea at Aberystwyth. The town was
named after its other river, the Ystwyth, which has a more
or less parallel course about 5 miles to the south.

The Severn gathers and grows in these wild, wet hills of Mid Wales,
and its many tributaries - Dulas, Clywedog, Carno, Rhiw, Vyrnwy
and countless tiny streams, deliver sparkling clear water. Some of
the lowland tributaries in Shropshire - the Perry, Tern and others
are more variable although now generally good, but far downstream
just south of Worcester, the Teme flows into the Severn from the
west. Rising in the Kerry Hills just south of Newtown, the source
is only about 7 miles from the Severn. It is Grade A to just south
of Ludlow and continues as Grade B. This late, welcome refreshment
helps the Severn to remain Grade B. Towns all over the Midlands
draw water from the River Severn - Shrewsbury, Wolverhampton,
Worcester, Coventry, Cheltenham, Gloucester.

The plants and creatures to be found along the Severn are not as
varied as you might expect, but you will find one common plant of
wasteland growing in its natural habitat. Tansy is a tall member of
the daisy family, a strong smelling hairless plant, with dark green,
feathery leaves. It is very much at home on the alluvial banks of
larger rivers where it has yellow, button like flowers from July to
October. The flowers look rather like ox eye daisies without white
petals, and that is more or less what they are.

The Severn once had two species of fish which are now rare in Britain, the twaite shad and the allis shad. An attractive fish, the twaite shad averages 25 - 40 cm in length. It has a series of seven black spots along the side, black dorsal and pectoral fins, black tail and orange pelvic and anal fins against a silver background. The larger allis shad has fewer black spots. Both species live in coastal waters but return up freshwater rivers to spawn. As such, they are both susceptible to the effects of pollution and obstructions to their passage upriver. The allis shad disappeared from the Severn in the 1840s, but the twaite shad still has a run.

The pikeperch, or zander, has now reached the Severn, a large toothed predator from eastern Europe. It was brought to England in 1878 from Schleswig-Holstein and kept at first in isolated ponds. Its escape into East Anglian rivers decimated native fish stocks and it is now a pest. In some places the pikeperch has resorted to cannibalism. We hope this fish can be removed from the Severn before there is damage to its ecology.

The River Severn imports Welsh water and, in times of spate, Welsh topsoil, so the water is rarely clear. It has an unusually deep and narrow channel for a lowland river, but this is not surprising. Between wet and dry periods there is a 4.5m to 6m variation in level. In winter the Severn races past, brown and bursting, and in low lying areas runs over the fields. In summer it murmurs genially round riffles of clean, grey stones and you have to clamber down high banks to reach it. Low summer flows provide ideal conditions for the white flowering river crowfoot, water milfoil, perfoliate pondweed and fennel pondweed.

In flood the river puts down a thick layer of silt which acts as a fertiliser. This encourages docks, nettles and similar strong and common species but suppresses smaller, more interesting plants. The lower Severn valley is wildly fertile and there is intensive arable farming. Much of the natural vegetation along these flatter reaches has been lost because nitrate fertilisers washed from the fields have a similar effect to the silt.

One feature of the Severn is the many eyots or small islands. They tend to have more varied and healthy vegetation because they are less directly affected by fertilisers. If you could reach them you might find chickweed, black mustard, Himalayan balsam, mudwort, almond willow, osier, tansy, slender tufted sedge and reed canary grass.

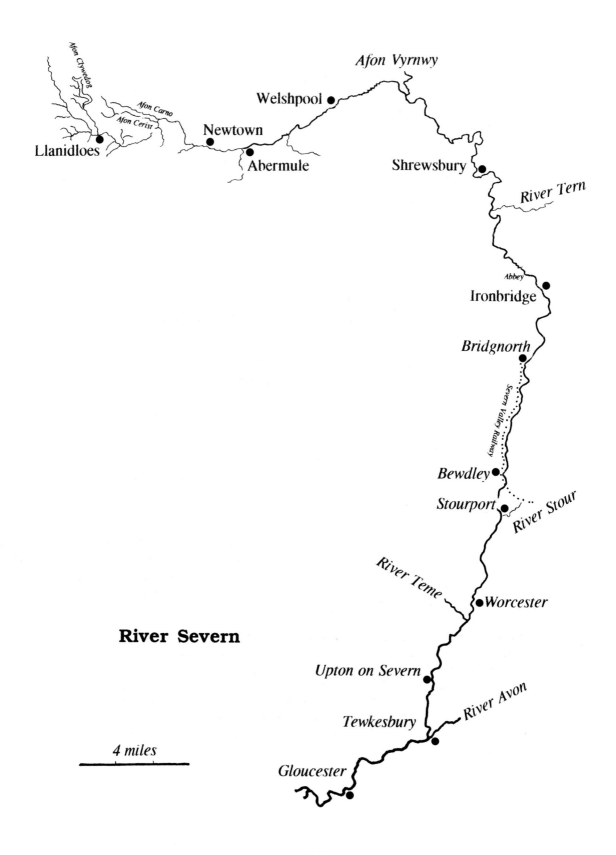

River Severn

Afon Vyrnwy

Welshpool

Newtown

Llanidloes

Afon Chwefog

Afon Carno

Afon Cerist

Abermule

Shrewsbury

River Tern

Abbey

Ironbridge

Bridgnorth

Severn Valley Railway

Bewdley

Stourport

River Stour

River Teme

Worcester

Upton on Severn

Tewkesbury

River Avon

Gloucester

4 miles

Many waterside plants are able to spread because their seeds travel downstream on the water. However, there is one plant that has spread upstream along the Severn, the introduced Himalayan balsam. This showy, pink and white flower has consistently spread upstream, no doubt helped by its alarmingly explosive seed pods.

In Shropshire, the Severn marks the dividing line between the flat northern plain and the southern uplands. A great part of the north and east of the county is in the rain shadow of these hills. If you like dry weather, the Severn Valley has the lowest rainfall in Shropshire; an average of 600 - 700mm in a typical year.

From Source to Shrewsbury

From the 600 metre contour on Pumlumon the Severn heads south-east through the Hafren Forest, where visitors can follow a Cascades Trail to see the best of the upland torrent. Within 10 miles the infant river has been joined by many tiny streams and the larger rivers, Dulas and Clywedog, so that by Llanidloes it has become a more powerful upland river.

In the 9.5 miles from its source to the confluence of the Dulas the Severn has fallen 432 metres, a rate of 45.5 metres per mile. None of our other rivers is so fast, though the Teme manages 37 metres per mile in its early stages. For comparison with a lowland river, the Avon manages 11.5 metres per mile in its first 6 miles, but over the next 4 miles falls only 5 metres per mile.

The Severn is obviously unpolluted at this stage, in fact the NRA do not grade the first upland section. However samples from above the confluence with the Dulas have shown acidification and lime granules were used to correct it, but this had ceased by 1993. The river is graded A as far as Shrewsbury.

The river rushes north-east over a pebbly bed, scouring beneath its banks as it swings to and fro across a deep, narrow valley. Nine more miles, and the valley broadens and flattens when it is joined by the Trannon and the Carno at Caersws. The rate of fall over the 9 miles from the Dulas confluence is 5 metres per mile, a very abrupt levelling off and comparable to the Avon in very different country. For the eight miles to Newtown it falls only 1.6 metres per mile.

With the Trannon comes one of the most potent and dangerous sources of pollution on the River Severn. The Avon Cerist rises about 4 miles west and passes through the site of the abandoned Fan Lead Mines (pronounced *van*). Mid Wales has the remains of many lead and silver mines, an industry which collapsed in the late 19th century, but this was the richest. It is now the most contaminated site in Wales with 16 acres of waste heaps releasing high concentrations of zinc, lead and cadmium into the river. Powys County Council and the Welsh Development Agency will divert the river round the site, install intercepting drains to catch further leaching and cap the tips with a waterproof cover. Fortunately the Cerist is soon diluted by the larger Trannon and in turn by the Severn, so that it does not reduce the quality of the main river.

The Severn is now a major river, but confined between hills to a direct course in a narrow valley for another 7 miles. Just north of Montgomery where the Rhiw and the Camlan enter, there is a great change of character when the Severn becomes a lowland river.

As if following the example of the lazy, meandering Camlan, which looks on the map like something from an anatomy text book, the Severn now winds and loops casually through the soft ground of a broad valley bottom. Just south of Welshpool the valley has room for the Mid Wales Airport. The rate of fall from Newtown has been 3.6 metres per mile, between the confluence of the Camlan and Welshpool it is 2.5 metres. The next section is almost level.

For the 15 miles between Newtown and Welshpool the river is accompanied by the 35 mile Montgomery Canal, a branch from the Llangollen Canal and part of the Shropshire Union Canal system. Built in 1821, it was in use for agricultural traffic until a major breach in 1936. Restoration efforts propelled by enthusiasts have been in hand since 1968, but official bodies are now committed to the Mongomery and there is little doubt that it will be restored.

Some 4 miles after Welshpool the Severn is still flowing north-east when it meets Offas Dyke, which follows it round an eastward bend some 7.5 miles to Crewgreen. The river writhes through this section like some mad intestine, looping and twisting through soft and easy ground. Offa, King of Mercia used the Severn here in his line of defence against the Welsh, in some places fortifying both sides of the river. The rate of fall since Welshpool has levelled off to .4 metres per mile and it hardly changes to Ironbridge.

At the small village of Crewgreen the Severn is joined by the River Vyrnwy, the largest tributary until the Team south of Worcester. The Vyrnwy flows in from the north bringing with it the boundary between Wales and England, which then follows the Severn for about about a mile. We would expect water quality in the Vyrnwy to be much like the Severn. The upper reaches are either Grade A or ungraded, but from the confluence of the Cain and the Tanat it is Grade B. The Severn has been Grade B since Welshpool but with the extra water from the Vyrnwy returns for a few miles to Grade A.

The border leaves the river near Pentre and the Severn heads for Shrewsbury. The town is some 10 miles as the crow flies (probably depends on the crow), but the river wanders an indecisive 20 to collect the River Perry. The Perry is so far only the second purely lowland tributary, rising near Gobowen and draining a largely flat landscape. All later tributaries are similar, except for the Teme.

Shropshire's county town stands on a rock around which the River Severn curls in great loop. It is a natural defensive position with only the narrow neck needing to be covered by a castle. The river provides excellent fishing with salmon, dace, chub and bream according to season. The water now becomes quality Grade B and remains so until the confluence of the Avon.

Shrewsbury to the Tern

Beyond Shrewsbury the Severn retains the looping, lowland character which it took on near Welshpool and continues south-east, past the National Trust's Attingham Park at Atcham. Near the proud, wrought iron park gates, two bridges carry the old route of the A5 across the Severn. The graceful five arched, stone bridge with an elegant humped crest was built in 1769-71 by John Gwynne, a founder member of the Royal Academy. The old bridge also has non human admirers because for many years it has housed a colony of hundreds of house martins.

A later bridge carries the modern road, and as you whiz over in a car, seems quite in keeping. But if you stop and look (better not) it is a crude, concrete mock up from 1929. The surface of the material has weathered badly, revealing nobbles of aggregate, and the proportions are mechanical. Look below the road deck to see the worst, the piers and arches are simple reinforced concrete in the style of the time. It is like someone wearing a powdered whig and braided frock coat over tracksuit bottoms and trainers.

Also at Atcham is a Georgian Inn called the Mytton and Mermaid. The Mermaid is a large sculpture in the stable yard. The Mytton was Mad Jack Mytton, an early 19th century squire and MP. He was a little eccentric. Among his many recorded escapades he once set fire to the tail of his shirt to cure an attack of hiccups. The hiccups went, but he got third degree burns.

The Severn at Atcham is notoriously liable to flood. These level fields can lie for weeks under sheets of still, brown water with stag headed trees standing like ghosts. The river pours south down its main channel, full and fast and dangerous, pushing desperately under the bridges and drowning the cutwaters.

Along the Tern

Just before the River Severn reaches the Roman city of Wroxeter, the Tern flows in to join it through the parkland of Attingham House. Its headwaters are 30 miles north, just beyond Market Drayton and quite close to those of the (Staffordshire) Sow which flows towards the Trent. This landscape is pockmarked by the effects of past glaciation, shown by the numerous small ponds. Through this green and level dairy farming country, the Tern is little more than a stream.

Market Drayton is an old town which has grown considerably over the years and claims to be the home of gingerbread. (A rival to Ashbourne?). The river here is still insignificant as it heads for Ternhill Barracks beside the A41. But soon it picks up the Bailey Brook and many other little streams, and has grown surprisingly by the time it reaches Stoke on Tern.

Running south through an agricultural landscape dotted with long disused military airfields, the Tern passes Eaton on Tern and heads for Great Bolas. This is flat, flat country and the straight blue lines on the map show a typical drainage pattern of many ditches and tiny streams. They do not quickly join to become big ones because there is not enough fall to the ground to run them together.

It may not have much to do with the river, but in derelict looking buildings on the Eaton airfield is a firm called Shelley Signs. The name may not be familiar, but they make most of the interpretive signs seen at nature reserves and tourist attractions throughout the country.

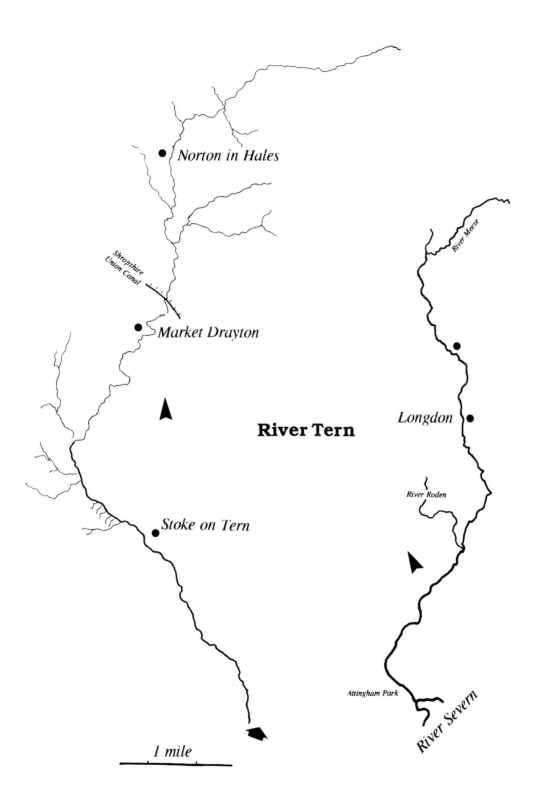

Norton in Hales

Shropshire
Union Canal

Market Drayton

River Tern

River Meese

Longdon

River Roden

Stoke on Tern

Attingham Park

River Severn

1 mile

Just south of Great Bolas the Tern is joined by the River Meese, not to be confused with several other rivers of this name. The Meese is a more substantial small river which drains much of the country north of Newport. This is slightly more hilly than the flat, airfield country. More or less following the line of the Shropshire Union Canal there is an almost imperceptible ridge, one side of which drains towards the Severn, the other towards the Trent.

The Tern has become a reasonable sized river by the time it reaches Longdon on Tern and begins to turn more westerly past the sugar beet factory at Walcot. Here it is joined by the River Roden from the north which runs via Stanton upon Hine Heath and Shawbury and close to Moreton Corbet Castle.

It is now only a couple of miles to the Severn, much of it through the deer park at Attingham. Unlike the Severn, the Tern passes close to the neo classical, late 18th century mansion. Like other rivers flowing through the parkland of great houses, the owners used it as a scenic asset. This is true of all the really gorgeous parts of the Upper Avon, and at Attingham we have the usual ornamental bridge.

The water quality of the Teme starts and ends as Grade B, reflecting its lowland origins, small flow and course through an agricultural landscape. A section near Market Drayton comes down to Grade C but the Tern recovers.

The confluence with the Severn is close to the A5, the Roman Watling Street from London to Holyhead. About a mile downstream is Wroxeter, one of the most significant sites of Roman Britain.

Tern to Ironbridge

The Romans called it Viroconium Cornoviorum, and Wroxeter was first used by the Roman military in AD 50. Its position on the east bank of the Severn gave it a strategic importance in conquering and controlling the central Marches. Work began on building the town in AD 60, it developed into a prosperous centre and remained so until a decline from around 250. Remains include part of the massive bath wall, one of the biggest pieces of Roman civil masonry in Britain.

Below the confluence of the Tern the landscape continues flat to Wroxeter. Then the land on either side of the Severn starts to rise and the river falls into a more defined channel.

Near Eyton on Severn, the river is joined from the west by the Cound Brook, which rises a few miles away in the Dorrington area and passes through Condover and Cound. Despite the name and short length, it carries a surprising amount of water because it drains the foothills of hilly south Shropshire. The Severn rolls on past the village of Cressage where the convincingly classical looking road bridge is a concrete mock up, but much better than at Atcham.

In the 15 miles from Shrewsbury, the Severn and its landscape have changed very little, but it is no longer a tortuous lowland river. From Cressage, small hills have been piling up on either side. After running alongside some parkland at Leighton the river flows on to Buildwas where great masses of gravels and sands built up during the complicated geological events which formed the Iron-bridge Gorge (see below). The landscape and the valley have now quite changed as the valley floor is squeezed into a narrowing gap.

Buildwas means the building (gebyldu) on damp soil (waesse), which is rather an understatement of the fabulous abbey by the banks of the river. Founded by Roger de Clinton, Bishop of Coventry and Lichfield, it was built around 1150 for the Cistercian monks.

The valley is now dominated by a modern monument, for just down-stream of Buildwas the Severn provides water for the Ironbridge Power Station. The vast pink cooling towers seem to fill the western edge of the Gorge, and above are the immense tree clad slopes of Benthall Edge and Tick Woods

The river has travelled some 48.5 miles from Crewgreen when we last commented on the rate of fall, and has dropped only 20 metres. This is a rate of .4 metres per mile, though in places it is slightly greater. The Severn is falling less quickly than the Avon north of Evesham and continues to do so, which surprised us.

Ironbridge Gorge

The creation of the Ironbridge Gorge was a major geological event at the end of the most recent Ice Age, about 12 million years ago. Until then the Severn flowed north from Welshpool towards the Dee estuary, but as more and more ice melted and dropped its burden of rock and sand this outflow became obstructed. The increasing volumes of melt water had nowhere to go, so began to form a series of lakes.

There were lakes in the Telford and Newport areas. The ice dammed lake in Coalbrookdale overflowed at Lightmoor and considerably deepened the Coalport Brook. But it was obstructed again by ice causing Lake Coalbrookdale to overflow towards Ironbridge. Water fell 50 metres in a mile as it plunged down to the Coalport Brook, and the power of this enormous flow started to gouge out the gorge.

At the same time as Lake Coalbrookdale was lowered, it expanded in area to cover the land as far as Buildwas so forming Lake Buildwas. While all this was happening, retreating ice around Newport caused a lake to form there too, the water building up against the higher ground to the east. This overflowed towards Gnosall in Staffordshire at about 95 metres above present sea level. However, as the ice continued to melt, Lakes Newport and Buildwas joined.

This temporary but mighty glacial lake was called Lake Lapworth by Professor Wills of Birmingham University. At its maximum the shoreline was 90 metres above sea level and the water covered the area from Newport to Shrewsbury, west to the Welsh border near Melverley and north to Wem. The summits of sandstone hills stuck out above the surface like many little islands.

Because the outlet at Ironbridge was 5 metres lower than that at Gnosall, the water flowed towards Ironbridge. Otherwise we might be talking about the Gnosall Gorge. Eventually Lake Lapworth overflowed and exploited the earlier work of the Coalbrookdale Brook to complete the Gorge. The released water was able to flow towards Bridgnorth to join the Avon river system and hence out to the Bristol Channel.

Ironbridge to Bridgnorth

The Ironbridge Gorge was birthplace to the Industrial Revolution, but unless you visit the museums and use your imagination, it is difficult to visualise the industry, dirt and pollution which once afflicted the valley. Today Ironbridge is a world heritage site with monuments and museums managed by the Ironbridge Gorge Trust. Squeezed between steep wooded slopes, it is a neat little town, a charming, untidy collection of industrial villages with humble brick houses clinging to hillsides near small factories. It has a careworn look, but has relaxed in graceful retirement as a tourist centre, complete with landscaping and traffic calming.

Abraham Darby's bridge of 1778 was the first iron bridge in the world, and since the properties of the material were hardly known it was built on the same principles as a stone bridge. Now it seems as beautiful and improbable as a barleysugar castle and is open only to pedestrians. On the riverside and close to the Iron Bridge, is the Museum of the River, the only one of its type we know and well worth a visit. A magnificent model of the river in 1796 shows the view actually visible downstream from the museum windows, with tiny houses, factories, trows, lighters, kilns and furnaces.

Also visible in the museum are marks showing the depth of flooding by the Severn. As late as 1960 it rose about a metre above the valley road, but in 1795 almost three metres.

The long industrial history of this area leads people to think that the name Coalbrookdale refers to past mining, but it is a corruption of Caldebrook, meaning cold brook valley. The name only became famous outside the area after Abraham Darby founded the Coalbrookdale Company in 1708.

The river had a definite influence on Matthew Webb, to whom there is a memorial in Coalbrookdale Church. There have been many other more ephemeral memorials, for he was pictured in Victorian bathing dress on certain boxes of matches. Born in 1848 in Dawley, he was taught to swim in the Severn. A few years later his swimming had developed sufficiently that he was able to rescue his brother from the river. Webb joined the Merchant Navy and became famous when he dived overboard in heavy seas to rescue a rating and was awarded the medal of the Royal Humane Society. He went on to swim twenty miles of the Thames from Blackwall Point to Gravesend in under four hours and became the first man to swim the English Channel. He drowned trying to swim the rapids under Niagara Falls.

Jackfield was full of families who earned their living from the river and seems to have been a rowdy place. A commonplace book kept by a barge owning family between 1828 and 1836 records incidents of violence, slander and theft. But Jackfield became famous late in the nineteenth century for decorative tiles. High quality clays were locally available and there was cheap coal to fire the kilns. Messrs Maw and the firm of Craven Dunhill turned out millions of tiles in thousands of designs for floors, walls, fireplaces, hallways, the fronts of pubs and shops, for town halls, hotels, railway stations, banks, swimming pools, palaces and churches.

The Severn at Bridgnorth in the summer of 1995

The hulk of the Arley ferry off Bewdley quay

At Coalport the river is flowing south-east, still in its deep, wooded gorge. The road here crosses the Severn by a graceful, modern cable stayed bridge with a single tower on the west bank. About one mile further and the Severn makes a decisive and final turn to head a little east of south, and hardly varies in direction for the next 45 miles to Tewksbury.

The river still runs between steep wooded hillsides as it reaches Apley Forge. Here the hills on the east bank retreat for a while at Apley Park, giving way to the broad and rather dull plain which reaches away east towards the catchment of the Trent. But within a mile the hills close in to form the wooded Apley Terrace. The Severn valley continues deep and often wooded, and although the land to the east falls somewhat south of Kidderminster, it has this character for the next twenty five miles south to Holt Heath. The river is now broad and majestic, flowing directly without extravagant loops.

About a mile upstream from Bridgnorth the River Worfe flows in from the east bank. It rises as a series of streams around the Shropshire villages of Claverley, Chesterton, Pattingham and Albrighton, all draining the land west of the catchment of the Smestow Brook which joins the river Stour. The streams merge near Wyken, then pass through wooded, undulating countryside around Rindleford for a couple of miles to join the Severn.

Bridgnorth to Bewdley

The Severn enters Bridgnorth beside the main A442 road and under an immense sandstone cliff. The soil formed by the brown sands in this area were some of the most favoured places for early settlement and sedentary agriculture. For this reason Bridgnorth has for many centuries been an important river crossing. Once a major river port, it is divided into Low Town by the river, and High Town perched on a red sandstone ridge above.

Telford's massive bridge was the only vehicle crossing between Coalport and Bewdley until recently, that is, in about nineteen miles of river. And like his next big bridge downstream at Bewdley, this one was grossly overused by modern traffic until both towns acquired bypasses and new bridges.

Nearby is the steepest cliff railway in Britain which carries
passengers up a forty five degree slope in cars which resemble 1930's
buses. In historic High Town is a Town Hall on stilts straddling the
street, Telford's St Mary Magdalene Church (there are not many
churches built by engineers) and an 11th century castle. Its ruins
include a precariously leaning tower, the result of battles during
the Civil War when the town was besieged by Parliamentary forces.

Bridgnorth was a centre for clothing and hat manufacture and later
engineering. Like all these riverside towns, the Severn was its main
source of transport and evidence of its importance can be seen in
the mooring rings fixed to the river wall and the bridge. Teams of
men were harnessed together to draw the coal barges into the wharves.
Warehouses and pubs crowded the river frontage. During demolition
of a coffee factory on this site in 1989 the contractors found the
remains of a friary. They were preserved during the redevelopment
and can now be visited.

Flooding occurs in the Low Town. New houses nearest to the river
on the east bank seem perilously near the high water levels which
occurred in the winter of 1994/5. In the past we built with less
valour and more caution.

In the 12 miles or so from Buildwas the river has fallen 10 metres,
a rate of .83 metres per mile. The rapid flow is achieved more by
the volume of water than this gradual descent.

From Bridgnorth, the Severn continues through largely pastoral
country. There are occasional arable fields but the proportion is
strikingly low. There has been a riverside footpath on the west bank
from just south of Coalport, and from Bridgnorth you can walk both
banks. The banks fall and the hills on each side become more smooth
and rounded, but the valley is still very distinct between high
ground.

The Severn curves east, passing close to the folly of Quatford Castle
built in the 19th century by a local builder, John Smalman. A little
further downstream at Quatford itself is the 11th century church of
St Mary Magdalene. Closer to the river is the site of a real motte
and bailey castle.

Between Lower and Upper Forge the river returns to its southwards
course and meets the Severn Valley Railway. Running 16 miles
between Bridgnorth and Kidderminster, this restored steam railway

is one of the most beautiful in the country. The six stations are restored and painted in GWR colours, with old posters, milk churns, trolleys and piles of luggage. There are five viaducts, two tunnels and the beautiful cast iron Victoria Bridge.

Small streams rising near the base of Wenlock Edge gather to form the Mor Brook near Morville, a little west of Bridgnorth. The rise and fall of the ground is negligible, but one of them rises within three hundred metres of the headwaters of the River Corve, which flows south-west parallel to the Edge to join the Teme.

Flowing south-eastwards, it becomes a substantial stream within the couple of miles to Cross Houses, then runs through Thatchers Wood and under the Oldbury - Glazeley road. From here you can follow it by bridleway and footpath past an old mill to Upper Forge. Another mile or so takes the Brook to its confluence with the Severn.

The landscape west of the Severn now settles into a complex pattern of steep rounded hills and deep valleys. However there is an underlying system of ridges running parallel with the Severn. This explains why the Borle Brook rising at Upton Cressett within 450 metres of one of the streams that forms the Mor Brook flows into the Severn, while the larger Rea Brook rising only a mile or so west runs south to join the Teme.

On the east side the hills and valleys are on a much smaller scale with consequently smaller streams. A few run west into the Severn, but more trickle down into the Smestow Brook and the Stour.

Near Quatt, the Severn passes the grounds of Dudmaston Hall, a late 17th century house run by the National Trust. It contains a fine collection of furniture and paintings, with many watercolours and examples of botanical art and natural history. A lakeside and woodland walk runs through The Dingle. The lake is one of a series along the valley of a stream; another stream flows through The Dingle to join it before they enter the Severn.

From Dudmaston downstream, the east bank is wooded for a mile to the Severn Trent water works at Hampton Loade. From the river, the ground rises in gentle undulations reaching 100 metres in about a mile. The other bank is a landscape of hedgeless open fields through which the railway runs, but the ground rises in much the same way.

A lane from the main road runs down to the east bank at Hampton Loade; another ends at Hampton on the west bank. Between them is a ferry operated by two sisters who have run the service since the 1950s. You may summon them by ringing a bell on a riverside post. Their craft is like a large punt and operates as many Severn ferries once did. A cable runs across the river between two stanchions. The boat is attached to it by a second cable which slips along the first on a ring. By swinging the rudder, the bow of the ferry is headed into the current which moves it across the water suspended from the fixed cable. A similar but much larger ferry at Arley worked until some fifteen years ago when it was replaced by a steel footbridge. The Hampton Loade ferry is the last of its kind in the country.

There is no human settlement for the next couple of miles as the river banks grow higher and steeper. The valley bottom is deep between high ridges at the Severn Valley Country Park which was opened in 1992. The vegetation near the river is thick and green and normal for the Severn Valley. Up the steep slopes it has triumphed by growing through thin black grit, for the site on both sides of the river was recovered from the waste tips and rail sidings of the Alveley and Highley Collieries which closed in 1969. The concrete bridge over the river used to support an aerial ropeway carrying coal to the washeries and the railway. The strange sloping site and its odd mix of acid and alkaline minerals supports a rich variety of wildflowers and butterflies.

Nearby is the small settlement of Stanley. On the west bank and high on a crest above the river is Highley, the miners village. To the east on the opposite crest is the more rural settlement of Alveley. From Stanley to Upper Arley there is little but fields and woods, the banks rising steep and green and cropped by sheep. Riverside paths follow both banks with the railway to the west.

At Arley the road ends at the river, but the ferry has gone and you must use the tubular steel footbridge. This object, like electricity pylons, is an engineering achievement but a scenic disaster. Otherwise, Arley is lovely and one of the spots most visited by people from the Black Country and Kidderminster. On the east bank is a pub, the church, a cafe, a post office, a quay and slipway, a huddle of houses and grand Arley House with its arboretum. On the west side is another pub and many people's favourite railway station.

This is the start of the Wyre Forest, with Eyemore Wood reaching almost two miles up the ridge on the east bank. Most of the forest is on the west side and only reaches down to the river at Seckley Wood, about a mile downstream.

The cast iron Victoria Bridge carries the railway across the river. When built in 1861 by the famous contractor Thomas Brassey, it was the greatest cast iron span in the world. Now it is a graceful monument, though we preferred the former green livery to the GWR buff and orange. Here photographers have the rare opportunity of snapping a steam train reflected in the water. Beyond the bridge, two sharp turns in the course of the river make room for Trimpley Reservoirs to be squeezed between rail and water. Opposite is Seckley Wood.

The Trimply Reservoirs supply Severn water to the local area of Worcestershire. Just downstream a mighty blue brick and steel aqueduct carries the Elan Valley supply to Birmingham.

From Folly Point, river and railway straighten again and head for Bewdley. Woodland is never far from either bank, although the east side is lined (infested?) with numerous chalets. About .75 miles from Bewdley the Dowles Brook joins the river from the west. Rising as several streams around the western fringes of the Wyre Forest, it flows through the heart of the woodland joined by tiny tributaries from from north and south. It never becomes a big river but once powered four watermills and forms the boundary between Shropshire and Worcestershire. Near the Severn it is bordered by the Fred Dale Nature Reserve, run by the West Midland Bird Club and Worcestershire Nature Conservation Trust. Here kingfisher, dipper and grey wagtail may be seen along the brook, with pied flycatcher, redstart, wood warbler and numerous other birds. With its more secret reaches far into the forest, Dowles Brook can claim to be one of most important wildlife habitats in the Midlands. We said a great deal about it in *Midland Woods & Forests*, so we will not bore you with more in case you go out and buy the book.

The valley here is still narrow, but there are no longer ridges of immense hills on either bank. At Bewdley Thomas Telford's three arched bridge spans the river, the first in the 12 miles since Bridgnorth. The name derives from beau lieu, meaning beautiful place. Today its trade revolves around tourism, but the past was very different.

Edward IV granted Bewdley a Royal Charter in 1472 and the town was soon trading in many exotic goods - cotton, tobacco, sugar, tea and slaves - thanks to its river links with Bristol and the sea. But it also carried more mundane cargo - leather, skins, wax, corn, timber and coal, many of them local products. In the 15th century firewood was shipped from Bewdley to Worcester and Gloucester.

The men of Bewdley were skilled at handling their flat bottomed trowes, or barges. They had to be tough, needing to fight off pirates anxious to plunder their cargoes, and press gangs sent upriver to take men off to the Napoleonic wars. The river is no longer navigable to Bewdley. For craft with more than minimal draught the limit is a shoal about a mile south at Blackstone Rock. Even so, canoes and rowing boats use it and there is an annual coracle regatta. Beginners learn to make a coracle on a course at Bewdley Museum, then get the chance to see if it floats.

Bewdley's river frontage is a picture postcard view on a summer's day, but residents know that appearances can be deceptive. It regularly makes the news when heavy rains burst the Severn's banks and flood the town. In winter fogs, with ice swirling down the racing brown river, it can be bleak place.

Bewdley to Worcester

The Severn flows on below the steep slopes of Ribbesford Woods on the west bank. Apart from the huge pink sandstone outcrop of Blackstone Rock, the east bank is now low, level and sandy, and the landscape rises only gently far from the river.

Stourport on Severn is about 3.5 miles downstream, a distinctive little town. From the river one first sees rows of moored boats; small cruisers and narrow boats from the canals and broad beamed river craft. Here is the first riverside park and playing fields, set off by a dignified but sporty cast iron bridge. Big passenger cruisers can be hired at Stourport for scheduled trips, or boats charted for a night time sail with traditional jazz and beer.

Just below the bridge is a funfair, and perhaps this best illustrates the modern character of Stourport which is not short of pubs, amusement arcades and chip shops. It would be interesting to know by just what social and economic mechanism this little brick Georgian town became a plastic Blackpool. Just on the outskirts is Hedstone Rock, in which you will find some caves to hide.

Stourport exists only thanks to James Brindley and the Staffordshire & Worcester Canal. A solitary inn stood here until the canal linked the Severn with the Trent & Mersey Canal. The terminus was complete by 1776 and a new town became the busiest inland port in the Midlands after Birmingham. Carpet manufacture in nearby

Iron bridges on the Severn - graceful and intricate.

Top: Holt Fleet bridge carries the B4133
Bottom: Footbridge at Bevere Lock

Kidderminster with brass and iron foundries, barge and boat building were among the local trades. These days the broad and narrow locks are still at work and the basin is a busy jumble of narrowboats and every kind of cruiser. The town's Georgian character was, in a strange way, preserved by the railways. By removing the canal traffic further development became pointless, and so Stourport is a museum as much as a resort.

Stourport is where the Stour meets the Severn at the end of its short journey from the Black Country. The next main tributary is the Salwarpe 8.5 miles away, and the next town is 12 miles off at Worcester.

Immediately downstream from Stourport and on the east bank, comes the great sand and gravel hill called Hartlebury Common. These 215 acres of dry heathland with a crest 36 metres above the river, were designated an SSSI in 1955. The Common was shaped by the River Severn as a series of gravel terraces. Windblown sand accumulated and was stabilised by gorse and broom on the upper plateau and heather on the lower terrace. Lowland heath is rare habitat in the Midlands, the other main example is Cannock Chase, so the Common is managed to maintain its present character. In the past this was done by grazing sheep and rabbits which kept down bracken, broom, birch and gorse. But farmers now need better fodder for their stock and rabbits have been reduced, allowing a shrub layer of trees to develop which would in time become woodland. In effect, a human workforce now does the grazing.

The floor of the Severn Valley from now on is wider than it has been since the Ironbridge Gorge. Small hills roll on either side and some-times close in on the river. From the water one's impression is of pretty and well wooded banks in hilly country.

At Lincomb is the highest lock and weir on the Severn. There are six in all to Gloucester - Lincomb, Holt, Bevere, Diglis, Tewksbury and Gloucester. In the section on Navigation of the rivers we mentioned that they could accommodate craft up to 5.5 metres in beam and 27.1 metres long. For people accustomed to narrow canal locks they look enormous. The six locks raise (or lower) craft through a total of almost 13 metres.

At The Burf is an isolated pub, but the Severn rolls on past Shrawley Wood, the most important ancient lime wood in England. Its northern boundary is formed by the fast flowing Dick Brook, quite a short stream which flows for much of its journey in a steep sided wooded valley. It was canalised in the 1800's by Andrew Yarranton who used flash gates to allow barges up the Brook to the site of an iron furnace. This is thought to be the first such commercial plant in the country, and the work on the Brook the earliest canalization of its kind. Sandstone walls and copings can be seen where the gates stood. At a later date a flint mill was built on the Brook to service the china industry, but was later moved to Worcester to form the beginnings of the Royal Worcester Porcelain Company.

Two miles downstream are Holt Fleet and Holt Heath with the first river crossing since Stourport, and these tiny settlements probably exist only because of it. No doubt at one time a ferry, it is now a handsome Victorian cast iron bridge. There are just a couple of houses near the river, and on our visit at the end of winter in 1995 the saturated sandbags round the doors showed the reason. There is a big pub and a cafe/restaurant, but the hamlet of Holt Heath is on higher ground almost a mile to the west.

The river flows on down a wooded valley for a couple of miles and there are no settlements on the river until Worcester. It is quite striking that the small villages nearby, such as Bevere and Northwick, sit cautiously back on ground a little above the valley floor. Such facts say a great deal about the history and habits of a river.

The Severn bypasses Ombersley, heading towards the A449 a little south of the village. Across the road is the 16th century Hawford Dovecote owned by the National Trust. You can visit on foot during the summer for a small fee.

Nearby, the Severn is joined by the wildly meandering River Salwarpe. This is one of several modest rivers rising from the ridge across the south of Birmingham and the Black Country, comprising the Lickey Hills, Waseley Hills and Clent Hills. From the north side comes the Stour which joins the Severn, and the Rea and Cole flowing to the Tame and Trent. The Salwarpe rises in the Lickey hills as the Battlefield Brook. After an inauspicious start it flows by the M5 before entering Bromsgrove, which it once flooded. Near to the Avoncroft Museum it picks up another small stream before heading on to Stoke Prior.

At Upton Warren an impressive nature reserve of the Worcestershire Nature Conservation Trust is marked by a plantation of broadcasting masts. The reserve is based on a couple of pools caused by subsidence following salt extraction. The most obvious interest is

The handsome cast iron bridge at Stourport on Severn

Worcester's city centre bridge with
church, cathedral and old warehouses

the birds, but the site is recognised for its selection of coastal plants which grow thanks to a brine spring. Each year the reserve records about one hundred and twenty species of birds, including tufted duck, ruddy duck and great crested grebe.

Bypassing Wychbold, the Salwarpe continues towards Droitwich, picking up another stream from the north. Droitwich is unique among European spa towns for being a brine spa. This incredible liquid contains more than 2 pounds of salt per gallon, far more concentrated than sea water. Unlike other spas, visitors do not drink the water, which is probably as well, but float weightlessly in the warm bath at Victoria Square. Built in 1985 it is the only spa treatment facility built in Britain this century. Droitwich Lido is also Britain's only inland, outdoor, salt water swimming pool.

At Droitwich the River Salwarpe flows through the town beside the Droitwich Canal, and they continue in company through the village of Salwarpe. The river writhes madly through a delightfully pretty valley on its last two miles to the Severn. There is a Salwarpe Valley Nature Trail; get details from Tourist Office in the Droitwich Spa Heritage Centre which also has a good exhibition about the town's history and the salt industry.

Half a mile further down the Severn is Bevere Island, one of the river's natural eyots. Next to it is the lock and the weir, a sheet of smooth, brown water skidding over the rim and crashing into foam.

The river rolls on towards Worcester, between the racecourse and the cricket ground, under the lofty iron railway bridge, under the classical stone road bridge built in 1791 and past the cathedral. Upstream of the road bridge the river is inaccessible, and nearer the city centre both banks are plaugued with traffic. Here the Severn has been channelled and banked into a dull, brown canal.

Immediately south of the bridge though, and Worcester begins to treat its river as an assett instead of a traffic obstacle. A riverside walk runs past the cathedral and rows of small houses to Diglis. On the west bank are recreation grounds.

The cathedral has dominated the skyline for more than 900 years. Here you will find medieval cloisters and the notorious King John's tomb. A ferry crosses from the Cathedral to Chapter Meadows in the summer months, river cruisers sail from North and South Quays and you can hire small boats for a DIY trip. Try not to compare yourself with the canoe and rowing club members who skim past.

A circular walk follows the Severn from South Quay by the Cathedral to Diglis canal basin. It returns along the canal to the Commandery, used in 1651 as the headquarters of Charles II during the Battle of Worcester. As the river leaves Worcester it is joined by the River Teme in an immense floodplain of flat, green meadows, the site of the Battle. You can learn the full story at the Commandery where the Civil War Centre has an award winning audio visual display.

Near the Ketch Inn on the A38 is a new roundabout, and a high, new embankment heads west across the battlefield. Overlooking the scene from higher ground by the road junction is a viewpoint with information boards and maps. They have been defaced by some brainless wonders, which makes them difficult to understand, but you can still plot the dispositions of the Royal and Parliamentary forces. The Civil War Trail will lead you on a two mile walk around the key positions of this decisive battle. We add a little more in the chapter on the River Teme.

From Bridgnorth the Severn has travelled about 31 miles. It has fallen 16 metres, a rate of .5 metres per mile. This compares with .83 metres further north, and is still less than the Avon north of Evesham.

Worcester to Tewksbury

The Severn now heads in a straight line for Kempsey. A footpath still hugs the east bank and several more pay visits to the west side then stop dead, a sure sign of ferries. There is no road crossing in the ten miles to Upton on Severn.

Kempsey is a village of mainly modern houses with terrific views of the Malvern Hills. The Severn flows between broad green banks and looks, strangely in view of the differences between, not unlike it did 30 miles upstream. However it is now flowing through a broad plain in a low lying landscape and swings freely to and fro. A footpath follows the east bank faithfully to Upton on Severn.

Entering Upton by road you pass markers showing the depth of flood water, and the town's whole existence and history have been tied to the river. There was a ferry but no bridge until 1605, when it was the only one between Worcester and Gloucester. Since then there have been many, all to be replaced by the present steel and concrete job which leaps the Severn in one powerful stride.

Upton is a pleasant Georgian town which was once a river port.
It is the first town since Worcester and the first of this size and
character since Bewdley, with which it has features in common.
Upton's main landmark is the tower of the old church. It stands
alone since the building of 1754 was replaced by a new church in
1879. The frivolous cupola replaced a spire and is much more fun.

Downstream of Upton, the Severn plain spreads miles wide to the
mound of Bredon Hill in the east and the ridge of the Malverns in
the west. The river meanders less now, it is too big to bother and
rolls ponderously on.

The Severn brushes past Tewksbury and is joined by the Avon
which does flow through the town. The smaller river does nothing
for water quality in the Severn, though it remains Grade B. In the
15.8 miles from its confluence with the Teme the Severn has fallen
only 6 metres, a rate of about .4 metres per mile.

At Gloucester the Severn becomes tidal, and at Minsterworth at
certain times of year you can watch the famous Severn Bore from
a bank by the church.

There are other rivers that have periodic tidal waves, but the Severn
Bore is probably the most famous. It occurs at high tides in the
Severn Estuary which can rise as much as 14.5 metres, the second
highest in the world. Bores are formed when the incoming tide is
forced up a narrowing channel with a rising bed. The effect in the
Severn is to produce occasional Bores 2 metres high, but they are
affected by winds and the volume of water flowing downstream. The
Bore moves upriver at about 10 miles per hour as far as Gloucester.
The National Rivers Authority publish a leaflet explaining the Bore,
with tables showing the times when they may be seen at various
places.

Downstream the river broadens and the meanders grow bigger. On
the east bank is the Wildfowl Trust's Slimbridge centre, to the
west the ancient Forest of Dean. On beyond Sharpness, beneath
the Severn Bridge and past the docks of Avonmouth and the great
river reaches the sea.

River Stour

A confusing family of streams runs down the north-eastern flank of the Clent Hills, passing through and around Uffmoor Wood towards Halesowen. Another set gather in the undulating country further west near Frankley and the M5, and they also make for Halesowen. One of the first group rises near St Kenelm's Church which has a holy well, and we would like to claim it as the source of the River Stour. Given the convention that the source of a river is the furthest tributary from the mouth, it could as easily be a trickle starting from a pond on the 230 metre contour near the M5, but this is the Illey Brook. Not that St Kenelm seems to have much influence on the 24 miles of the River Stour.

The Clent Hills group of streams meet near the Grange, Halesowen. The Frankley group meet at Halesowen Abbey, a little known ancient monument without public road access. People seem to reach it by trespassing from nearby public footpaths. The Premonstratensian canons who built the Abbey used the Stour to supply fish ponds; the remains can still be seen. Both streams plunge separately under the Halesowen bypass and into the urban area, but do not actually meet for another mile and a half beyond the A458.

At this stage some 3 miles from the source of the longest stream, the Stour has fallen 104 metres, a rate of 34 metres per mile. The water quality so far has been Grade C, and in the conurbation recent improvements allow it to retain this quality almost to Lye. It then falls to Grade D for a mile, then to E.

The whole of the source area often surprises visitors. The Clent Hills and the area round the Abbey ruins are not just pleasant, in a urban fringe sort of way, this is idyllically pretty countryside by any standard. The streams which will shortly form the Stour run from this setting into the south-western edge of one of the greatest conurbations in the world. The Stour is the river of the Black Country. No wonder that when it emerges at Amblecote, Stourbridge some 7.5 miles on, it is a different creature.

There are little rural intervals. One comes immediately after the Halesowen bypass when the Clent stream passes a housing estate. Here there are willows and alders, celandine and wild garlic for a few hundred yards, but both streams soon vanish into black culverts under the inner ring road.

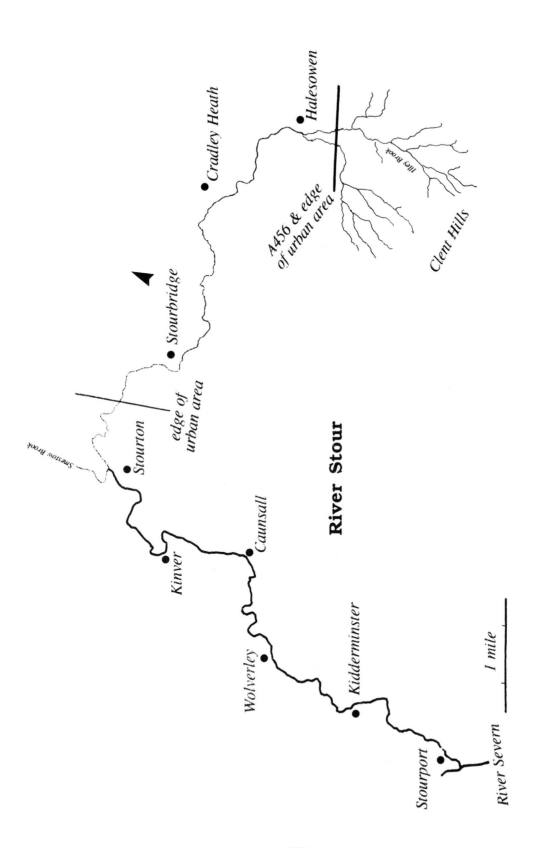

River Stour

Cradley Heath

Halesowen

A456 & edge
of urban area

Illey Brook

Clent Hills

Stourbridge

edge of
urban area

Stourton

Smestow Brook

Kinver

Caunsall

Wolverley

Kidderminster

Stourport

River Severn

1 mile

(77)

Compared with other rivers in this book information on the River Stour was easy to come by, largely thanks to a research project and catchment plan drawn up by the National Rivers Authority. To include all the absorbing information it contains would take about a hundred pages. We were alarmed that if it weighed and cost so much you might not buy the book, so we have just cribbed some of the main points.

Study of the Stour

The River Stour and its tributaries drain 373 square kilometres of the Midlands, from Wolverhampton in the north to Stourport in the south, and from Frankley in the east to near Shatterford in the west.

The River Stour rises in the Clent Hills and its main tributary the Smestow Brook, in Wolverhampton. The Staffordshire & Worcester-shire Canal follows them closely on its way from the Trent & Mersey Canal to the Severn at Stourport. It was an early "contour" canal built by the pioneer James Brindley which followed river valleys to reduce changes of level, and hence expensive locks and excavations.

Thirty five per cent of the Stour's catchment is urban, much of it in the Black Country, whose heavy industry had and still has a horrible effect on the quality of the water. Further downstream at Kiddermin-ster there is carpet making, some light industry and a sugar beet plant.

Outside the towns most of the catchment is agricultural with some pasture and areas of intensive arable land. There is a great deal of woodland, particularly around Kinver, and most of the area is Green Belt.

Compared to other parts of the region rainfall in the Stour catchment is low, averaging 700mm a year. After evaporation there is only around 240mm left to find its way into the soils and the river. In dry years the flow of the Smestow Brook and Stour can be cut by half, when more than half of the flow at Stourport may be treated sewage and industrial effluent. There are nearly fifty consented discharges of industrial waste in the area, most directed through drains to Severn Trent treatment works. The most significant is treated effluent from potato processing and metal finishing. There are also discharges from quarries, waste disposal sites and swimming pools. Individually they probably would not have a serious impact on the river, but the combined load from such a big urban area adds significantly to the amount of toxic metals and suspended solids in the water. Pollution may also seep unplanned into the river from waste disposal sites and scrap yards. Until 1976 they were poorly controlled with very little in the way of anti pollution measures. Dumping in the Black Country was, historically, so widespread that there can be few areas free of it.

Rural areas have not suffered to the same extent, but two areas have taken generations of sewage sludge. In the Whittington area between the Staffordshire & Worcestershire Canal and Iverley there was a vast sewage farm. Walkers attracted by the exciting contours of the small, sandy hills and the two bridleways, are first surprised by the strange smell. Often they do not comment, thinking it might be emanating from one of their party. Usually the odd blue brick structures which dot the fields making gurgle and splat noises explain the situation. There was similar dumping at Wombourne. All this is being phased out, but it will take up to thirty years for concentrations of nitrates and chlorides to wash out of the local groundwater.

Much of the central part of the catchment lies on the Sherwood Sandstones, a highly permeable aquifer used a great deal for public, industrial and agricultural water supplies. By contrast, the Coal Measures to the east provide only a small quantity of water. All of the 190 megalitres per day extracted for drinking comes from 22 boreholes. Only some water for industry, amenity lakes and cooling is taken direct from rivers and streams.

These sandstones have long been an important source of sand and gravel and there are many quarries. Clays and marls for brick making are extracted around Dudley and Wolverhampton and there are many old coal mines. Any or all of these may affect the river as sources of pollution or through changes in water levels caused by pumping in the quarries. Water levels can also change quickly after storms because of run off from the urban roads.

The River Stour is not the most ecologically important of the region's rivers. Water quality is relatively poor and the banks often steep sided. However in its early stages it is one of the few natural habitats in the urban area. Downstream in the central rural reaches, earth banks provide nesting places for kingfishers which are quite common.

The Stour and its tributaries provide suitable conditions for a range of fish, but the variable water quality severely restricts the range of species. Brown trout have occasionally been recorded near the confluence of the Blakedown Brook and the Stour, but are usually found only in the Hoo Brook. There are gudgeon through much of the catchment, with pike and dace. However roach, eel and chub have been found along some stretches, with bream near Stourport. Stickleback, bullheads and stone loach are found everywhere. The Staffs & Worcs Canal between Swindon and the River Severn is a designated cyprinid (non salmon and trout) fishery.

Halesowen to Stourton

Sneaking through the centre of Halesowen and past Halesowen College, the Stour turns west to form the boundary between the Boroughs of Sandwell and Dudley. As the river heads towards Cradley it passes a sequence of factories and forges, the essence of the Black Country.

The Stour emerges briefly to cross Haden Hill Park, then at Lye just east of Stourbridge there is a deep curved valley which is a successful small nature reserve. But the industrial scene runs on to Lye, then the valley opens out a little around Bouchall and Clatterbatch.

The Black Country is quite a hilly place and before it was so densely built over, the whole of this south-western corner of the West Midlands would have been wonderfully pretty. It is a northward extension of the Clent Hills, rising to 200 metres in the centre of Dudley and 270 on the Rowley Hills. Try to imagine the Stour flowing down a green valley winding between rounded hills.

Just north of Stourbridge town centre, the Stourbridge Canal starts and follows the river valley. River and canal flow side by side through a pleasantly green urban section to emerge quite suddenly into rural Staffordshire. In the 6.7 miles from Halesowen the river has fallen 76 metres, which might surprise even local people, giving a rate of 11.3 metres per mile. Water quality is Grade C until about half way through the conurbation, but after a Sewage Works near Lye it falls to Grade E and remains so to the Severn.

For the next mile river and canal flow through a pretty rural valley between woodlands and meadows. The Stour then wanders off to the north to find the Smestow Brook and the canal heads south-west to

Stourton. This reach of the river is almost level, with a fall of no more than .5 metres per mile.

Stourton is a small village which has developed around a series of transport junctions, and just to the north the Smestow Brook and the Stour meet in a delightful wooded setting. Close by is a large lake joined to the Staffs & Worcs Canal, apparently once intended as the junction with the Stourbridge Canal. For some undiscovered reason it was decided to move the junction after the lake had been built, and the canals now meet about half a mile downstream.

The Smestow Brook

Like the Stour, its main tributary the Smestow Brook is ecologically impoverished, but it is an important natural feature in the Wolverhampton area. The Staffordshire & Worcester Canal is also pretty poor, having too high a density of suspended sediment to allow much plant growth, but where the two run parallel the marshland between can be invaluable.

Running between Wolverhampton Racecourse and Aldersley Stadium, the Brook flows for two miles through Valley Park, a walking and picnic area along the trackbed of the disused Great Western Railway. It is well wooded and more than one hundred and eighty species of plants have been recorded, including musk mallow, mousear hawkweed and storksbill.

Passing a small nature reserve off Aldersley Road, the Brook reaches Compton where it flows between the Bridgnorth Road and the Staffordshire & Worcester Canal. To the north is Wightwick Family Park, and on the hill a small woodland bird sanctuary.

At Wightwick the Brook flows past Wightwick Manor (National Trust), built in 1887 for Theodore Mander by Edward Ould of Liverpool, and paid for out of the profits of Mander's Wolverhampton paint business. Outside it is timber framed, brick and tile. Inside it feels comfortably homely, yet is decorated and fitted with the highest quality of Pre Raphaelite and William Morris art, swirling floral wallpapers, embroidery, rich carpets and tiles.

Flowing out of the town, the Brook reaches a level, agricultural countryside. The valley is a just a shallow undulation with the Brook at 83 metres running not far below the higher points at 100 or so. It leaves the canal to wander away west, past Trescott, through Seisdon, to Trysull. It is still a very small river of the sort that looks like a ditch and gets a culvert rather than a bridge, but until 1940 it powered Trysull Mill. This old building still has its iron water wheel with gearing and three pairs of grinding stones. Nearby All Saints church includes an inscription about a foundation made by John Rudge in 1725. His bequest provided one pound a year to the sleep rouser, who awoke members of the congregation who fell asleep during the service and cleared the church of dogs which became a nuisance.

Quietly, the Brook becomes more busy. It is responsible for a bed of osiers at Trysull and wanders round more freely. About half a mile on it turns through ninety degrees to head south, neatly taking a line parallel to the Staffs & Worcs Canal. Skirting the western edge of Wombourne, it dodges through small industrial estates and old sand quarries.

Wombourne is a sprawling village, both rural and urban, with shops and houses gathered round an attractive green. It was a well established village at the time of Domesday and obviously much smaller, but one would have seen the predecessor to the present church and perhaps even then they took sand from the small hills to the west.

At Wombourne, the Smestow Brook is joined by the Wom Brook. Starting as a series of streams flowing in from Penn and Sedgley, it swells the Smestow Brook to more forceful dimensions. One of the headwaters is the Penn Brook which flows across the rural and wildlife rich Penn Common, a part of Penn remarkably different from the northerly suburban area along the A449.

The Brook rejoins the Staffs & Worcs Canal at Botterham Lock and they continue together until the Brook joins the River Stour.

Sedgley sits astride the watershed which divides the Black Country from the countryside to the west. Here a stream rises and heads off the four and a half miles to join the Smestow Brook south of Swindon. Around the source of the stream has developed Cotwall End Nature Centre. As well as the natural habitats afforded by its setting, the Nature Centre has some aviaries, a walled garden and a fox's lair which can be viewed through a window.

Swindon had an iron forge before 1668, when it was leased by the ironmaster Thomas Foley. Even earlier, in the 1620s, there was an iron furnace here burning coal rather than charcoal, over 100 years before the method was rediscovered by Abraham Darby at Coalbrook dale. Whitesmithing, or making edge tools from tempered iron, was widespread in Staffordshire during the 17th century. Both Swindon and Himley had blade mills to finish the local products.

The landscape and the valley have now started to change. Sandy hills in the west are getting bigger, and in the east the ridge forming the west side of the urban area is closing in. The valley is becoming steadily narrower, more wooded and more distinct and attractive.

A cluster of Roman camps at Greensforge north of Stourton has no obvious connection with the river but such sites were often placed close to a water supply.

The Smestow Brook picks up the Dawley Brook from the east, a short stream draining the Kingswinford area. From the west comes the Spittal Brook which is fed from several streams draining the Enville district. In the last 2 miles of its course it forms the Checkhill Bogs. This truly remarkable place can easily be seen from several local lanes. It looks very wild and primitive with a tangle of trees growing in an expanse of semi stagnant water, scattered with giant clumps of rushes and sedges. Although the trees look craggy and ancient, these woods probably developed from old osier beds.

The Bogs are dominated by a mixture of alder and crack willow. Some of the alder has been coppiced in the past, whilst fallen crack willows have sprouted a thicket of suckering branches. Several other willows grow here, including the bay willow at the southern limit of its English range. In summer high nutrient levels encourage the growth of nettles, and the beautiful but rather too common Himalayan balsam adds a splash of pink. In places you can find wetland flowers like meadowsweet, gipsywort, bittersweet, marsh marigold, water mint and water forget me not.

Wet, humid woods like this are great hunting grounds for specialist naturalists. The abundance of dead wood adds to the interest and provides perfect conditions for many mosses, liverworts, fungi and insects. It is a lovely place to see the midges and mosquitos, if you like that sort of thing. This is a type of woodland under increasing threat and very restricted in Staffordshire.

Crossing the Stour -

at Halesowen Abbey -

and by the canal near Cookley.

Stourton to the Severn

Stewponey is a small western appendage to Stourton, no more than a cross roads. Here the Stourbridge to Bridgnorth road meets one from Wolverhampton to Kidderminster. Just to the north the Smestow Brook has joined the Stour, and the Stourbridge Canal has met the Staffs & Worcs. If all this put you in a social mood, convivial humans can meet at the Stewponey and Foley Arms, a huge, comfortable pub which serves food, Bank's beer and on some days, live jazz. Silly jokes aside, the name is supposed to be derived from Estepona, the home town of the Spanish bride of a soldier returning from the Peninsula War. The Foley bit comes from the famous local family of early ironmasters.

The Stour skirts all this meeting business by cringing to the west and tumbling over a weir under Stourton Castle. The Smestow Brook has made it a much bigger river, but no sparkling stream. Water quality varies between C and D so its waters do improve the Stour, but not enough to raise it from Grade E. It flows on, tortuously, through Dunsley to Kinver, always close now to the Staffs & Worcs Canal whose relative straightness emphasises the bends.

Kinver has a quaint(ish) high street, a selection of pubs and ales and Kinver Edge. The village is well known for its rock houses cut into the soft sandstone, and some were occupied well into the 1950's. The most famous are at Holy Austin Rock on the northern side of Kinver Edge.

Less obvious today are the rock houses of Gibraltar Rock close to the Staffordshire & Worcester Canal by the Vine Inn, which were used by the men who worked the canal and river. The wharf at Kinver Lock was in almost continuous use and extra labourers waiting to load the cargoes could rent the little houses for one shilling (5 pence) a week. Damp made them less comfortable than those on the Edge, so by the mid 1880s they were no longer rented out, though boatmen continued to use them for a while. Years ago moisture caused the rock to crumble so there is almost nothing left.

Entering Worcestershire just south of Whittington, the Stour and the Staffs & Worcs Canal follow one of the most beautiful small valleys in the Midlands. There are frequent sandstone cliffs and the valley is quite narrow. The small hills on either side roll scenically to form those delightful contours so typical of this part of the county. Canal and river wind on to pass Cookley and Wolverley and reach Kidderminster.

At Wolverley the river has travelled 6.7 miles from the confluence of the Smestow Brook, and fallen 14 metres, a rate of 2.1 metres per mile, compared with .5 metres between the conurbation and the Brook.

Here the Stour valley begins to broaden out for its confluence with the Severn, and Kidderminster town is built at a natural constriction in the floodplain. The carpet industry was originally driven by water power and placed buildings across the entire width of the plain. Serious flooding over two hundred years has caused much damage, but the decline in the use of water power has allowed many old sluices and mill weirs to be removed, so easing the water flow.

Downstream from Kidderminster the river and canal separate a little, allowing a series of important wetlands to develop between them. Of special interest is the valley between them near Wilden Pool and Hoo Brook, near Stourport. This stretch of river to Stourport was made navigable by earthworks following a statute of 1666, but the banks were destroyed in a flood in 1680 and never restored.

The urban area tends to disguise the fact, but the Stour valley has suddenly broadened into a sandy plain almost three miles wide. One of the locks on the canal is called "Falling Sands Lock", suggesting the difficulties which the navvies experienced. However, unlike many rivers the fall of the Stour does not decrease as it nears its mouth, but increases in its last 6 miles from Wolverley to fall 16 metres at 2.6 metres per mile.

Stourport was nothing more than a sleepy village before the coming of the canals in the 18th century. Then its strategic position at the point where vessels bound for the Trent and Mersey and Birmingham left the Severn encouraged Stourport to develop into a major port. In fact, the town holds a unique claim to fame. It is the only British town which owes its existence entirely to canals. When canals were superseded by railways the importance of Stourport declined, to leave (behind the facade of bingo and chip shops) the fine example of a Georgian town we see today. Nevertheless, in its day it was the second ranking Midland port after Birmingham.

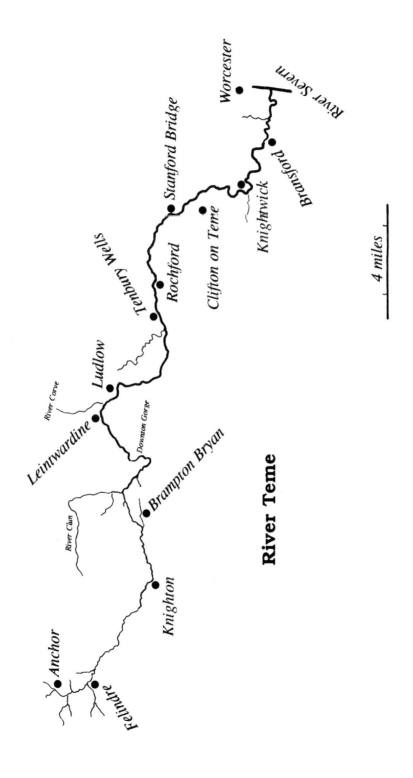

River Teme

River Teme

The River Teme rises half a mile south of the Kerry Ridgeway at 450 metres. Within a mile to the west are the sources of the River Mule, which flows north-east into the Severn, and the Ithon which heads south into the distant Wye. This is high, hilly, green, sheep country, heartlifting and remote. The nearest town is Newtown, 4.5 miles to the north, the next is Llanidloes over 10 miles west.

The Teme trickles south down the flank of Cilfaesty Hill to Cwm Gwn to start its 70 mile journey to the Severn. Within a mile and a half, it is flowing quickly down a narrow and steep valley. After another 2 miles the Rhuddwr Brook joins from the north and soon, at Felindre, the Cil-owen Brook makes it an upland river. In 5 miles it has fallen 182 metres, a rate of about 37 metres per mile.

In the next 10 straight miles south-east to Knighton, the Teme is confined by the hills into a narrow valley, but swings to and fro across the floor. Small tributaries run in by the dozen from the surrounding high land, so that it swells mile by mile. Passing through Knighton, a small border town amongst wooded hills, it is crossed by Offa's Dyke, then swings east. Here the character of the Teme is still of a tumbling, upland river, though over this section it falls 98 metres at a reduced average rate of about 9 metres per mile.

From Knighton to Bucknell the Welsh/English border more or less follows the river, though not so closely as boundaries often do. Before Lingen Bridge it heads off south towards Presteigne. A change has been developing since Knighton and the valley had opened, but quite suddenly it becomes broad and level as the Teme runs east past Brampton Bryan to Leintwardine.

The contrast appears from the rate of fall. In the 6 or so miles from Knighton to Brampton Bryan the river falls 44 metres, some 7.5 metres per mile. In the 2.5 miles to Leintwardine it falls only 8 metres at 3.3 metres per mile.

Leintwardine was Roman Bravonium and here the River Teme is joined by the River Clun. The Clun like the Teme, starts on the Welsh borders, but for much of its course it winds and twists extravagantly. In the last five miles to Leintwardine it becomes quite intestinal and very much a lowland river. The River Clun passes through Clun (itself), Clunton, Clunberry, Aston on Clun and Clungunford; some sort of record. The river drains all the northern part of the Teme's catchment, which is steep and wet country so it brings down a lot of water. As it flows, augmented, under the old bridge at Leintwardine, the Teme has become a large and powerful river.

From Leintwardine the combined waters of Teme and Clun head south-eastwards for a few miles along a looping reach called the Leintwardine Fishery, where it collects several small streams. After negotiating a series of small meanders within a broader one, a change of direction becomes obvious as the river flows north-east into the Downton Gorge. This is a broad and level section in which the Teme falls only 2 metres in nearly 5 miles, a rate of .4 metres per mile.

Like many rivers in this region, the course of the Teme was radically altered by the last ice ages. It once flowed south from Leintwardine to join the River Lugg, and eventually the Wye. However ice blocked its exit north of Aymestry and the build up of water formed a lake in the Vale of Wigmore. Eventually this overflowed to the north, cutting the spectacular Downton Gorge through the 300 metre high ridge of Bringewood Chase. The sediments formed in the lake still determine the local soil; you can easily see its outline from maps and the local topography.

In the 4.25 miles through the Gorge to Bromfield where it meets the River Onny and turns south east, the river falls 30 metres, a rate of 7 metres per mile.

Flowing on to the north-east through woodland and parkland brings the Teme close to Bromfield, a hamlet on the River Onny. The church of St Mary stands close to its confluence with the Teme. It used to be part of a priory, some of which was converted to a house. In 1672 when the tower of the priory became the chancel of the church, the extraordinary decorated ceiling was painted.

A diversion down the Onny

The River Onny starts in a number of streams rising in the hills to the north of Bishop's Castle, some of the better known being

Stiperstones and Corndon Hill. The main headwater is the River West Onny which rises on the fringe of Stapeley Hill to the east of Priestweston. Immediately it forms the border between England and Wales. The border hugs the river through Whitegrit and down beside the A488. After a couple of miles the border continues down a tributary towards the wooded Iron Age hillfort at Snead.

The West Onny heads east, picks up more streams from below Shelve, then passes between Black Rhadley Hill and Cefn Gunthly. Flowing south along the foot of Linley Hill, it soon reaches Linley followed by More, where it is within 100 metres of one of the streams which form the Camlad, a lazy Clun-like tributary of the Severn.

Once more the West Onny changes direction back to the south-east. Near Eaton it is joined by the East Onny which follows the valley between The Stiperstones and The Long Mynd. Through aptly named Bridges, it continues past Wentnor and Whitcot. At Hardwick another stream flows in from Norbury just before the confluence with the West Onny.

Shortly after the confluence, the Criftin Brook also joins from the north. The new and augmented River Onny flows through Plowden, around the southern end of The Long Mynd to Horderley. To the north are the wild exposed slopes of Long Mynd, to the south the steep and wooded slopes of Plowden Woods. This valley is the Onny Gorge and was created by the ice age. Until its passage was blocked at Church Stoke the upper reaches of the Onny flowed into the Camlad. A lake then formed between Lydham and Long Mynd which overflowed to cut the gorge.

The next reach follows the A489 to just beyond the A49 at Cheney Longville. Here it collects the combined waters of the Lakehouse Brook, Eaton Brook, Byne Brook and Quinny Brook from the north side of Wenlock Edge, then turns south for Craven Arms.

Just beyond Craven Arms the Iron Age hillfort of Norton Camp commands the east bank. Opposite is the amazing Stokesay Castle. Despite its name it is not a castle, but a fortified 13th century moated manor house which was altered in the 17th century. It is the only known and complete example of its age and type in existence. You enter through an Elizabethan gatehouse which leads first into a courtyard. There are two towers linked by a great hall, solar wing and passage.

Tenbury's bridge - half sandstone, half concrete

Eastham Bridge over the Teme near Newnham Bridge

Another 5 miles and a few more streams brings us to Bromfield and the Teme, where the valleys of both rivers merge into a wide plain

To Ludlow & Tenbury Wells

It is less than 3 miles to Ludlow but another tributary joins the Teme from the north. The headwaters of the River Corve gather themselves from near Bourton on the south-east side of Wenlock Edge. By Shipton several streams have already been captured but the river is still little more than a brook. However, it already occupies the broad valley of Corve Dale between the Clee Hills and Wenlock Edge.

By Beambridge more streams have been taken up and the river is looking more substantial. It runs down a wide, flat and lonely dale as it heads for Culmington. Soon there is the confluence with the Pye Brook, one of the headwaters of which is the Clee Brook.

At Clee St Margaret this little stream runs along the village street for at least fifty metres and needs an unusually long ford. Clee St Margaret sits beneath the 540 metre Brown Clee Hill. It is a tiny place with its church and its Norman doorway just six feet high. From the church there are views down Corve Dale along which the ever growing Corve turns south for Stanton Lacy.

Past Ludlow racecourse, the river heads for the western fringes of the town, joining the River Teme before it swings under the massive red stone ramparts of Ludlow Castle. The Teme has now absorbed most of the rivers of mid Shropshire.

There was no real settlement at Ludlow before the Norman Conquest, though there may have been a small agricultural community from Saxon times. The castle was founded by the de Lucy family between 1086 and 1094 and around it a planned town developed. Extensions to the castle obscured the original grid of streets and from 1233 the town walls were built. Medieval suburbs continued to grow until by 1377 it was 33rd in a list of English towns.

From the mid 15th century to 1689, the castle was the main centre of administration for the Council of the Marches and Wales, a commission set up by the Crown to dispense justice in the borders. This administrative role and flourishing cloth trade made Ludlow a

prosperous medieval and Tudor town. By the 18th century it
was a fashionable resort for the rich. Many local industries
declined in the early 19th century but this century has seen a
revival of tourism.

The River Teme loops south of Ludlow. Here Dinham Bridge
crosses with the main road to Leominster, Hereford and the
south. The river has levelled off and its fall from Bromfield has
been 3.3 metres per mile. The water quality of the Teme from its
source to about this point has been Grade A, but it now becomes
Grade B. Until recently it fell to Grade C between Tenbury Wells
and the Severn, but improvements now allow Grade B all the way.

After the 3.5 miles to Ashford Carbonell, the Teme starts a slow
turn east and the landscape changes. It is not so much hilly as no
longer flat, and small green hills begin to crowd the valley towards
Tenbury Wells. Near Burford House Gardens the Teme picks up
Ledwyche Brook, a substantial little river running from the east
of Ludlow and draining much of the east side of the Clee Hills.
The Teme has one more important river to collect.

To Rochford & Along the River Rea

Tenbury and Burford sit on opposite sides of the River Teme in
Worcestershire to the south, and Shropshire to the north respec-
tively. The county boundary follows the river for just over a mile.
Under the bridge it is all shoals and shingle and small grassy
islands. Take the slipway to the water on the Tenbury side to see
the curious angled bridge. Although it looks from the top like an
elegant Georgian structure with iron railings, the old sandstone
bridge was incorporated into a concrete imitation in 1908.

The Teme has fallen 26 metres in the 9.5 miles from Dinham Bridge
at Ludlow, a rate of 2.7 metres per mile, a considerable levelling
from the 7 metres per mile through Downton Gorge.

After some 3 miles of red soil and hopyards to just past Rochford,
the River Rea joins the Teme from the north. This starts life as a
series of streams rising in the undulating country to the east of
Brown Clee Hill. By the time they have reached Oreton they have
come together to form the Rea. Flowing south, the Rea takes in
small streams from the north corner of Titterstone Clee and from
the ridge to the east, which forms the west side of the Wyre Forest.

Near Detton Hall the Rea passes close to the site of a deserted medieval village before reaching Neen Savage, then Cleobury Mortimer.
Look for the twisted spire of St Mary's church. Closer inspection
will show that the walls are not all that straight either.

Skirting the edge of Mawley Hall on the fringe of the Wyre Forest,
the Rea adopts the complicated, meandering habit of lowland rivers.
Before Neen Sollars it briefly forms the boundary between Shropshire
and Hereford & Worcester, but soon loses it again. The countryside
is both friendly and exciting, with well wooded green hills dotted
with blissful orchards which burst with spring blossom.

The Rea valley is followed by the route of a disused railway which
crosses and re-crosses the river. Between Neen Sollars and Newnham
this also crosses a short but substantial tributary of the Rea, the
Mill Brook. It gains such a substantial flow in only a few miles by
carrying a great deal of the water falling on the steep slopes of
Titterstone Clee.

Quiet valleys & distant villages

From Rochford the Teme flows roughly east or south-east, dreaming
back and forth across its flood plain between hills spread with woods
and orchards. From the hills the valley looks amazingly deep.

The river passes close to but not through any villages until gets to
Stanford Bridge. Do not believe place names like Knighton on Teme
or Stockton on Teme. However, it is possible to walk some reaches of
the river, such as the footpath which leaves the A443 near Eardiston.
After crossing fields this soon brings you to the river bank, which
can be followed for around 3 miles to beyond Stanford Bridge.

Traffic now crosses the valley on an uncompromisingly modern bridge,
very light and graceful. As at Tenbury, the old bridge is not quite
what it seems. This one too was rebuilt in 1908 and the iron railings
disguise a concrete arch, though they made quite a decent shot at it.
Perhaps we might call it a misguided attempt to be sympathetic rather
than a cheap imitation. To judge from the remaining abutments, this
bridge replaced an older brick structure. But the river flows under
it anyway, lively and clear over a pebble bed and looking its
quality Grade B. It has fallen only 12 metres in the 9.5 miles
from Tenbury, a rate of 1.23 metres per mile.

The hills to the east are nearly 100 metres above the river and dramatically steep. They are part of that most exciting set of hills running almost 25 five miles from Bewdley in the north to the southern tip of the Malverns.

Again, the river avoids most settlements, including Clifton upon Teme, which is nearly 2 miles from the river on top of a hill. Bypassing Martley and skirting a hillside crammed with orchards, the Teme meanders towards Knightwick. Here it picks up a stream flowing in from Lower Brockhampton where the National Trust have a late 14th century moated manor house with a fascinating detached 15th century gatehouse.

Taking a great sweep, the river is soon flowing roughly south-east again to pass alongside Broadwas Court. The rate of fall from Stanford Bridge has been 1.33 metres per mile, almost unchanged from Tenbury. A mile or so to the south-west and crowning a hill of 140 metres is Ravenhill Wood, a reserve of the Worcestershire Nature Conservation Trust. A disused railway follows the river valley, leaving the mainline at Rushwick and heading west.

Leigh Brook

Between Broadwas and Rushwick is Leigh where the Leigh Brook joins the Teme. This stream has its headwaters to the west and flows through the Silurian rocks that run from the Malverns north to Abberley Hill. Two of its streams join at Longley Green, then flow north-easterly through hilly, wooded country. On a loop of the Brook at Alfrick Pound is another Worcestershire Nature Conservation Trust reserve, The Knapp and The Papermill.

This reserve is a Site of Special Scientific Interest acquired by the Trust in parts since 1968. It includes a range of wildlife habitats, a house, garden, old apple orchard, woodland, grassland and, of course, the Leigh Brook. There is a small visitor centre, wildlife garden and a nature trail.

The Leigh Brook takes most of the water draining the western side of the Malvern Hills. This is a large catchment area and the depth of water varies greatly depending with the weather. In times of spate the normally clear Brook becomes brown with soil washed from the surrounding land.

In the reserve the Brook is home to a wide range of water birds including kingfisher, dipper, grey wagtail, moorhen and mallard. There is a hide near a spot where kingfishers breed in most years, offering exciting glimpses of this most brilliant of birds. They nest in tunnels cut as far as six feet into a vertical bank. This gives some protection from predators, but rapid increases of water level in the breeding season can lead to the nest flooding. Since the mid 1970s mink have colonised this area. Look out for them as they are more likely to be seen in daylight than the native otter. If you are really lucky you might spot a water shrew.

The Brook was long ago diverted to serve a mill which worked until 1973. Nearby is the weir which has been in place for at least 200 years and you may be lucky enough to see trout leaping it. The only remnant of the paper mill complex is Papermill Cottage, which now provides accommodation for conservation work volunteers.

A big meadow on the reserve used to be called Great Epiphany because the rent was due at the church festival of Epiphany - 6th January. This also gives the name to the old bridge over the Leigh Brook, Pivany Bridge. In summer you can stand on it and admire the white flowered beds of water crowfoot. This is a relative of the buttercups. Although it has submerged leaves, it pokes its flowers above the surface so that they can be pollinated by passing insects. Other plants which you may see on the reserve include monkshood, wood goldilocks, leopardsbane, common gromwell, snowdrop, common and violet helleborine and greater broomrape. More than 100 species of birds and 160 species of moth have been recorded.

Several footpaths cross the hills, meadows, woods and orchards between the reserve and Leigh, giving many routes to the brook-side and a choice of five bridges by which to cross it.

To the Severn

The Leigh Brook joins the Teme by Leigh Court, where there is a riverside orchard and church. As the river heads for Bransford Bridge and the busy A4103, there is another opportunity to walk a riverside footpath. Between here and historic Powick Bridge the footpaths give only glimpses of the river.

Since Broadwas the valley has broadened and the landscape levelled off to become low and bland. Effectively, it ends at Powick Bridge and merges into the Severn valley, but even here the Teme collects a last tributary. Because of the low ridge on the Severn's west bank, The Laughern Brook runs south and parallel with the big river, yet less than a mile to the west.

On this plain between the two rivers was fought the Battle of Worcester. In August 1651, Charles, who had been proclaimed King Charles II at Scone in Scotland, crossed into England with a Scottish army of 17,000. Advancing slowly and harried by local militia, they marched through Warrington, Newport and Wolverhampton to arrive at Worcester on August 22nd, their forces reduced to some 12,000.

Cromwell assembled about 28,000 Parliamentary troops and moved from Nottingham. Charles relied on the defences provided by the Severn and Teme near Powick Bridge, but his rivals built a floating bridge across the Severn near the confluence. They could then cross the Teme on horseback at a ford south of Powick Bridge to attack the King's ill protected flank.

Charles watched the fierce battle from the Cathedral tower and noticed that part of the Roundhead right wing was isolated. He tried to take advantage of the situation, but his cavalry fled by the road to the north. Cromwell forced the Royalists back into the city where many were killed in the narrow streets. Charles fled, and for the next six weeks made his famous fugitive tour of the Midlands before escaping to France. This was the last battle of the English Civil War, because Charles II's return in 1660 was at Parliament's invitation.

Although now in the valley of the Severn, the Teme performs a last meander. Its loop is so contorted that the water is close to breaking through the neck of land to form what geographers call an ox bow lake.

Powick Bridge

River Avon

Born on a battlefield

The River Avon starts its 100 mile journey as a tiny stream trickling from the 185 metre contour near the centre of the village of Naseby. These are the Northamptonshire Uplands, a long continuation of the Jurassic ridge of limestone rock which reaches from the Humber to the Dorset coast. They reach no great height but the area does have an upland look, enough for us to say that our three main rivers, Severn, Trent and Avon come out of the hills.

Naseby is a little red brick village best known for its Civil War battle. Here on 14th June 1645 Oliver Cromwell's Parliamentary forces defeated those of Charles I and determined that the country would be ruled by an elected Parliament and not the King.

Two hundred and thirty years later there was another battle, this time over the rights of farm workers. The Union of Agricultural Workers had been formed two years earlier by the famous Joseph Arch, and in 1875 he spoke to two thousand people at Naseby. We meet him again downriver at his birthplace in Barford. In a more recent battle, the villagers have certainly lost. A campaign to stop construction of a link between the A1 and M1 Motorways has failed, and as we write (1994) work is well underway.

From Naseby the infant Avon is channeled round field edges, picks up another ditch and flows into the Naseby Reservoir serving the Grand Union Canal. It continues north-west for about 2 miles as a canal feeder stream to Welford Reservoir, then having contributed much of its water to the Welford Arm of the Grand Union Canal, it becomes independent.

The Avon passes the village of Welford under a neat sandstone road bridge by the Wharf pub and runs north-west beside the canal for a further 2 miles, forming the boundary between Northamptonshire and Leicestershire. The landscape rapidly loses its hint of upland character to become more typical of the arable Midlands. Just south of South Kilworth the river turns sharply south-west, a general direction which it maintains for the rest of its course to the Severn at Tewksbury.

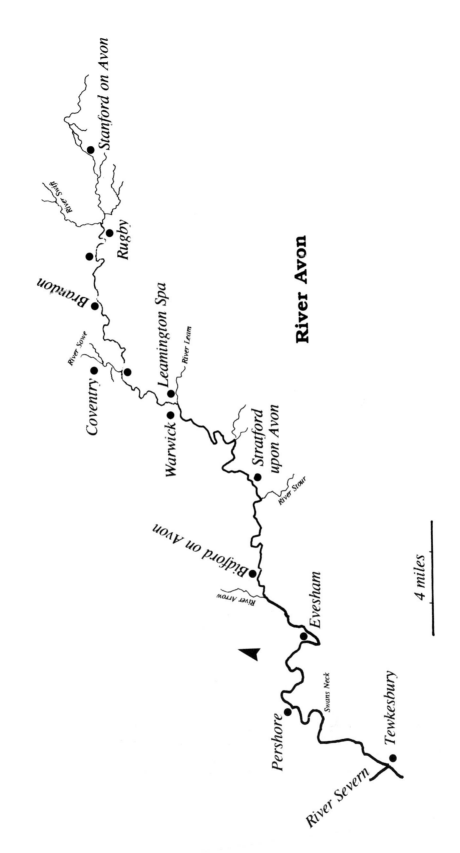

River Avon

Stanford on Avon

River Swift

Rugby

Brandon

Coventry

River Sowe

Warwick

Leamington Spa

River Leam

Stratford upon Avon

River Stour

Bidford on Avon

River Arrow

Evesham

Swans Neck

Pershore

Tewkesbury

River Severn

4 miles

In about 6.5 miles the Avon has fallen 65 metres, or nearly 10 metres per mile. In the next 6 miles it falls only some 26 metres, or 4.3 metres per mile, and will not run so freely again. The NRA grade water quality from the Naseby Reservoir as B, which it remains to Clifton on Dunsmore near Rugby.

Still marking the county boundary, the Avon flows in a shallow valley between low hills with distant woods, then through a sluice gate into Stanford Reservoir. The boundary line tacks about engagingly, as if lost in the deep water; presumably this was the original line of the river. This lake is a little over a mile long and supplies drinking water.

There is woodland beside the river as it enters Stanford Park, a mass of snowdrops in early spring, and you can see mallard, coots, mute swan and heron. Near the hall, the river has been dressed up as a feature and widened into a lake with a large island. However once under the road bridge below the Hall it drops the act and becomes a narrow stream again.

Although still clean enough to extract for drinking, the young Avon has already passed through some arable land to pick up nitrates and pesticides. The landscape ahead promises more of the same.

Stanford Hall has been the home of the Cave family since 1430, although the present building was only built in the 1690s. In the 1890s electricity was installed with the help of ferrets. A hole was made in the walls at opposite ends of each room and a ferret put into one of them with a flex attached to its collar. It rapidly made its way under the floorboards to the other hole to claim a piece of dangled rabbit.

Stanford Hall is in Leicestershire but the hamlet of Stanford on Avon at the southern tip of the grounds, is in Northamptonshire. St Nicholas's church, ignoring some nasty concrete pinnacles, is magnificent. There is a rich collection of medieval stained glass, seventeen hatchments, the most immense and vulgar monument you can imagine and well … go and see.

Stanford to Rugby

The Avon meanders away for a couple of miles across level, arable farmland and the county boundary follows. At Lilbourne the M1

*The Avon burbles under Lilbourne bridge,
with bailey in the background, if not motte*

The bridge and walkway to Little Lawford Mill

crosses the valley on stilts and a tributary flows in from Clay Coton. Immediately past the motorway viaduct are some unnatural looking mounds which are the remains of motte and bailey castles. King Stephen certainly had a castle here, held by Gerard de Camville. However judging by the mounds, now rather eroded by grazing sheep, there may have been more than one. Bubbling under the pleasant brick bridge, the Avon is surprisingly clear and deep, but water quality falls to Grade C in the next two miles and it must be affected by run off from the M1.

Flowing on towards Rugby, the Avon valley becomes wide and deep. After a mile and a half it reaches Dow Bridge and the A5, Watling Street, the Roman road from London to Holyhead. Here too, the boundaries of Northamptonshire, Leicestershire and Warwickshire meet and the Avon flows on into Warwickshire.

The river passes between Newton and Clifton upon Dunsmore to pass under the Oxford Canal in Rugby's suburb of Brownsover. It has so far been treated with respect, the valley is public green space and the watercourse, still only a couple of metres wide, is clear and green with plant life. However it has fallen only 4 metres in the last three and a half miles, near 1 metre/mile.

What has been a rural river flowing through an agricultural land-scape is suddenly transformed by two things. First the Clifton Brook and the River Swift join to make the Avon a strong, small river. Secondly, it is channeled between concrete banks to pass the GEC works. Drainpipes in the wall pour their contents into the river and there is little sign of vegetation. The Avon becomes a dead looking, urban river, but recent improvements allow it remain Grade C. By Little Lawford some two miles on it becomes Grade B to the confluence of the Sowe south of Coventry, when it crashes to D. The NRA delicately describe it as unsuitable for public water supply.

In the next two miles the river creeps dismally through the centre and suburbs of Rugby, takes in the produce of a sewage works and loops abruptly north through a poplar lined valley to the overgrown village of Newbold on Avon.

Its enticing name has not helped it resist suburbanisation, but high up on a sandstone rock Newbold has a pleasant setting, an attractive church, and a canal wharf and tunnel. Looping round Newbold, the river flows through a wide valley between sloping green fields, and passing under the cast iron footbridge to Long Lawford it (at least) looks attractive and rural.

River level is now about 80 metres, so through Rugby it fell by about 5 metres, a rate of about 1.3 metres per mile. This small increase in fall and speed is of some benefit to a small, newly burdened river, but not much.

Rugby to Brandon

The valley is less deep as the Avon runs on for a mile to Little Lawford. Here is an old water mill, now a farm, and two fords crossed by earth tracks. The upstream ford has a very long raised walkway (see photo), suggesting the extent of flooding.

There is precious little else here since the Hall was demolished in the 1790's, but there are remains of a fishpond and the stables have been turned into houses. The date on the building - 1604, is suspect. Experts think 1700 more likely.

The valley widens further and the land to the north flattens. After about 1.25 miles by road, or 2.5 by river because of another huge loop south, the Avon reaches Kings Newnham. The valley is now broad and shallow in rather featureless arable country.

Next to Newnham Hall stands a square, three stage Italianate tower built from the local limestone rubble with red sandstone quoins. It looks oddly Mediterranean, draped in ivy and standing here by the Avon. This is what remains of the church of St Lawrence which was probably built by the monks of Kenilworth Abbey. The nave and chancel were destroyed in 1794, the bells taken to St Mary's, Monks Kirby and the font stands in the garden of Newnham Hall.

In 1850 someone noticed that water drained very quickly from the former churchyard. Excavation uncovered a water filled underground vault containing several lead lined coffins. One held the body of Lady Audry Leigh who had died in 1640 before her 17th birthday. Others held the corpses of Francis Earl of Chichester, Lady Chichester, Lord Dunsmore and Sir John Anderson. A last coffin contained a headless body. Lord John Scott ordered the coffins to be resealed and replaced, and a zinc cover built over the vault.

Monks from Kenilworth created three stew ponds opposite the hall, which provided fish for days which the church had decreed would be meatless Today the ponds and the river are very popular with anglers.

The Avon continues the next 1.5 miles to Bretford much as it left Rugby and growing only slowly from the few small tributaries. The river hurries under the Fosse Way by a five arched sandstone bridge which has been heavily braced with steel rods and flanges to withstand modern traffic. Traffic lights limit the load to single file. This is another Roman road which runs in arrow straight sections between Exeter and Lincoln.

Within 2 miles the Avon passes beneath the Coventry to Rugby railway line and flows between the villages of Wolston and Brandon. The road bridge is an odd hybrid, grey sandstone piers and four brick arches. Between the river and railway are the rectangular earthworks of the thirteenth century Brandon Castle.

As you might expect from the landscape, the fall of the river has slowed. At Brandon bridge the level is about 70 metres from the 80 or so as it left Newbold on Avon, a fall of about .7 metre per mile.

Brandon Marsh

In the next 4 miles to Ryton Bridge on the A45 the Avon loops lazily through a gravelly, watery landscape. You would expect the change in river levels to be small, but it has come down to 65 metres over 4 miles, a fall of 1.25 metres per mile; slightly more than the last section.

A huge swath of ground on each side of the river is sand and gravel which has been quarried here for centuries. Brandon Marsh Nature Reserve is actually a series of old gravel pits. It is also the headquarters of the Warwickshire Wildlife Trust.

Local naturalists first took an active interest in the area in 1968 when they formed the Brandon Marsh Conservation Group. They worked for many years with the aggregate company, Redland, to monitor and conserve the wildlife. Their efforts were rewarded in 1981 when 54 hectares of the site were licensed to the Trust as a nature reserve.

Before gravel extraction Brandon Marsh was a series of riverside meadows. The gravel works and settling pits created much of the wetland, but the area has also been affected by subsidence caused by past coal mining at Binley. All this has created one of the most important wildfowl sites in the Midlands which has been designated a Site of Special Scientific Interest. The reserve is very varied, with tranquil reaches of open water, marshland, ditches, reedbeds, damp grassland, dry grassland, scrub, hedgerow and mixed woodland. One of the water areas is directly connected to the river.

The birds are the most obvious interest, especially water birds. Over two hundred species have been recorded including mallard, tufted duck, pochard, shoveler, coot, moorhen, Canada goose and great crested grebe. There are large numbers of the small duck, teal and both bearded tit and short eared owl are present most winters. The Trust has made a shallow scrape which is attractive to waders such as little ringed plover, redshank and green sandpiper. Nine species of warbler breed here, and sometimes even Cetti's warbler.

Studies of plants have identified more than four hundred and thirty species. There are plenty of sedges, rushes, reeds and willows. In early spring splashes of the bright yellow flowers of marsh marigold brighten many parts of the reserve. Later in the season there is yellow flag and sweet smelling, creamy flowered meadowsweet.

The diversity of habitats is important to the insects and mammals. Willows alone can support around two hundred and fifty species of insect including a range of brightly coloured beetles. The caterpillars of the colourful red underwing moth feed on the willow leaves at night, as do the yellowish green caterpillars of the poplar hawk moth.

Other invertebrates include several species of snail. You may find fragments of their shells by big stones which have been used by song thrushes to smash them open.

Voles and mice provide food for owls, whilst stoats and weasels themselves prey on other creatures. Rabbits are common and often nibble about on the banks of the pools in daylight.

The Reserve is open every day and has a network of paths, several bird watching hides, a nature trail and several interpretive signs explaining the main features. Get a booklet from the visitor centre.

Ryton Bridge to Stoneleigh

From some of the bird hides you can see the mass of the Ryton Car Plant beyond the trees. The Avon sneaks past the plant, collects from a sewage works, dives under the throbbing A45, slides around the back of an industrial estate, skirts Coventry Airport and totally avoids Coventry to reach the village of Bubbenhall. The valley has continued broad and level, with reeds growing in many of the meadows. There are more gravel and sand quarries.

However at Bubbenhall the church stands on a small hill above the river, which has become a little deeper and narrower. The footpath through the churchyard allows glimpses of the Avon through tall alder woods which are carpeted with thousands of strongly smelling wild garlic plants. These trees were coppiced years ago, that is, cut down to ground level and left to regrow as poles. However coppicing is no longer economic and clusters of stout trunks have developed.

Flowing on beneath Bubbenhall Bridge, the river is being gently confined by a slight rise in ground level to the north. Cloud Bridge at Stoneleigh is a composed, seventeenth century classical structure in warm red sandstone. Here the river banks are steeper with more trees, and the Avon seems to have resumed its rural character after the industrial areas near Coventry.

For the second time the Avon enters parkland, and as at Stanford Hall, gets the grand scenic treatment. After skirting the Massey Ferguson Training Centre and flowing serenely through a golf course, it passes under the medieval Stare Bridge to reach Stoneleigh Abbey and the National Agricultural Centre.

This beautiful limestone bridge has seven small, irregular arches, some round, some pointed, and of varying widths. The downstream face has similarly assorted buttresses. Stare Bridge now carries a footpath and the road passes by on a more suitable structure.

There are still some large oaks around, but nothing to suggest that the village and Abbey of Stoneleigh once stood at the heart of that densely wooded part of north Warwickshire called Arden. At the time of Domesday there were four miles of woodland supporting two thousand hogs and two mills. Over the centuries the forests were cleared so that today the Norman village church stands by riverside meadows grazed by sheep and cattle.

In the 19th century, Stoneleigh was a favourite destination of cyclists from Coventry who would line up their bikes by the Stoneleigh Arms (now Forsythia Cottage). On a Sunday morning in 1890, some of the cyclists called and whistled after Cordelia, daughter of Lord William Leigh. Sir William, Lord Mayor of London,

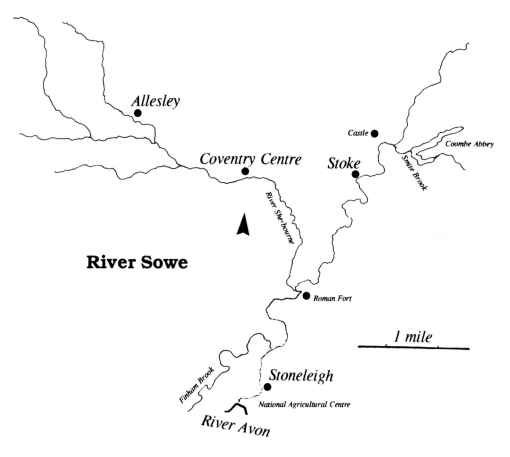

Allesley

Castle

Coombe Abbey

Coventry Centre

Stoke

Smite Brook

River Sherbourne

River Sowe

Roman Fort

1 mile

Finham Brook

Stoneleigh

National Agricultural Centre

River Avon

*Little Lawford Mill
is now a farm*

was so incensed that he ordered the pub to be closed and insisted there should never be another in the village.

Around the end of the 19th century the water mill on the Sowe was converted into the village co-operative. The proprietor, Jo Morris, acted as butcher, baker and transport operator, running a weekly service to Coventry which often included pigs and chickens among its passengers.

The Sowe joins the Avon just outside the village and on the edge of the Royal Showground which occupies much of the parkland of Stoneleigh Abbey. The Abbey was a Cistercian foundation which eventually passed to Alice, wife of Lord William Leigh.

River level where the Sowe flows in is about 53 metres, a fall of 12 metres in the 5.5 miles from Ryton Bridge. This is an increased rate of fall to about 2.2 metres per mile, and what you might expect from the slight changes in the landscape. It is beneficial bearing in mind effluent so far recieved and what is to come from the Sowe.

Along the Sowe

The Sowe is the Avon's first major tributary and drains the area north-east of Coventry. For a river which only becomes significant in the 7 or so miles from Coombe Abbey Country park on the City's eastern fringe, it brings an astonishing amount of water to the Avon. However, for most of its course the water quality is Grade C or D but falls to Grade E just before the confluence.

The Sowe is an entirely urban, or at least suburban, river since the main stream rises in Longford, north Coventry. From here it flows south-east through the suburbs to escape briefly into the countryside. Not far from this point are the remains of Caludon Castle which was crenellated during the reign of Edward I. It is owned by Coventry Corporation and can be visited at any time.

Other streams gather close to the junction of the M6/M69 and head south-west to meet the Sowe. Within half a mile they are joined by the slightly larger Smite Brook after it has passed through Coombe Pool in Coombe Abbey Country Park. By the time it has reached the road bridge on the A4082 and re-entered the City, the Sowe has grown enormously.

Passing between the districts of Stoke and Binley, the river heads around the southern fringes of Coventry to Baginton. This is a fascinating area with the remains of a castle (private and not accessible) and The Lunt, a reconstructed Roman fort which gives a vivid insight into military life two thousand years ago.

Meanwhile, the Sowe does what suburban rivers do, which is to provide a valuable green strip through the built up area and take the run off from roads and houses. The NRA study of the Severn tributary, the Black Country Stour, shows how its flow varies greatly between periods of low and high rainfall. Run off from roads, pavements and houses will either be a lot, or nothing, so this will always be a feature of urban rivers.

At Baginton the Sowe leaves town, and from the church a riverside footpath leads to Rennie's 19th century eight arched bridge at Stoneleigh. In this reach the Sowe collects an important tributary from the Kenilworth direction, the Finham Brook, which brings with it the products of a nearby sewage works.

Stoneleigh to Warwick

The Avon almost encircles Stoneleigh Abbey and the Royal Show ground, and another great meander takes it to Ashow. The church of this tiny, secluded village is twelfth century and stands on the riverbank at the end of the main street. It has a fine medieval roof and box pews. Next to it is a pretty timber framed cottage.

From the little footbridge, the river is visibly deeper, darker and more powerful than a few miles upstream, the work of the River Sowe. And now it has that dank, dead, smell of effluent which we have met only in the Black Country Stour, the Tame and the Trent. It will continue as Grade D to the confluence of the Leam.

A little downstream by the Leamington Spa road is a big hotel complex. From here a public footpath follows the river across fields to near Hill Wootton. A left turn takes you down a lane and over the river, to the main road by a large antiques shop. Across the road, more footpaths lead across the fields to Ashow, allowing a pleasant short walk. The landscape is gently undulating and quite well wooded.

Another large meander and the river reaches Guy's Cliffe. A cave in the cliff was retirement home for Guy of Warwick. You can obtain elsewhere details of this tedious and tendentious tale about a medieval thug. Briefly, his retirement involved living in the cave and not letting on to Mrs Warwick, who had been pining in the Castle for twenty five years. (Obviously another thicky.) It ends predictably when she hears that the old man is about to pop his clogs. Hurrying to the cave she, naturally, arrives too late and chucks herself over the edge, and has spent the last twelve hundred years wafting about the neighbourhood causing alarm.

Nearby at the Saxon Mill public house and restaurant you can have a peaceful riverside drink. The sandstone cliff rises to about 15 metres above river level and curves with the river for about half a mile. The land to the east rises but the valley is broad, and towards the south end of the cliff the river drifts off some distance to the east to enter the gap between Leamington Spa and Warwick.

From Saxon Mill you can cross the fields to the hamlet of Old Milverton. This tiny settlement is an estate village but seems popular with well known people. The parents of the politician Shirley Williams are buried in the churchyard, as are Sir George Catlin and Vera Brittain, author of Testament of Youth and women's rights campaigner. Beware opposite the Parish Room, the old barn bears the (illegally discriminatory) warning *"Man traps and spring guns on these premises"*

Flowing in a green valley between Leamington and Warwick, the Avon passes beneath Milverton Bridge. The original bridge of classical design has three broad stone arches, but the deck is now supported by a discreet modern steel and concrete structure. The river is deep and placid as, just downstream, it curves west into Warwick and the River Leam flows in from the east.

River level has fallen about 6 metres in the 7.5 miles since the Sowe. This is an average fall of 1.25 metres per mile, rather less than the previous section.

Down the Leam

The Leam rises between Helidon and Priors Marsden on the western flank of the Northamptonshire Uplands. Two streams start on the county boundary with Warwickshire, merge and head north-east.

Footbridge over the Leam in Jephson Gardens, Leamington Spa

*The classic view
of Warwick Castle
and the Avon*

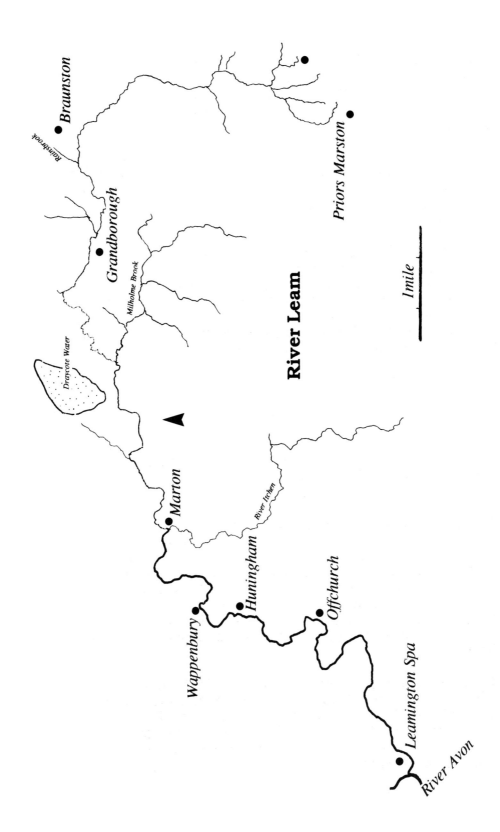

Within a couple of miles the combined stream starts to mark the county boundary until just west of the canal village of Braunston. The River Leam is a little more than a big stream, but it passes through a moderately hilly landscape and in places forms quite deep valleys.

In its 6 miles to this point the Leam has fallen 50 metres, that is, 8.3 metres per mile. By contrast it falls only 53 metres in its next (and last) 20 miles, a rate of .4 metres per mile. From Braunston the Leam becomes the archetypal lowland river, with a fall less than all the others in this book and its middle reaches the most tortuous.

After eight and a half twisting miles collecting minor tributaries, the Leam reaches Grandborough in Warwickshire where several large streams come together. Grandborough's chief claim to fame is its connection with rugby balls. Mr Harry Timms who once lived in the village worked at Gilbert's in Rugby where they were made. He took a great pride in his work and even after retirement could be seen stitching balls at his cottage doorway.

A mile and a half later the main contributor to the Leam flows in from the east, the Rains Brook, which drains the wide valley south of Rugby. Although it started in grassland the Leam, and more so the Rains Brook, have been passing through mainly arable farming country. They collect large quantities of nitrates which coarsen and simplify the species of plants that live beside them, and do not improve the water's drinking qualities. However the water of the Leam is Grade B until it enters Leamington and falls to Grade C.

As the Leam passes Kites Hardwick and the south end of Draycote Water, water is drawn into this big reservoir to supply the Rugby district. It flows on another two and a half miles past Leamington Hastings to Birdingbury. Here an unnamed stream from the south adds usefully to its volume. Next it arrives at Marton, where it is joined by the little River Itchen flowing in from the limestone country to the south, in fact from near Edge Hill which is part of the Jurassic Ridge. The Leam continues a much more significant small river.

The Leam maintains its curious habit of flowing past, not through villages, at Eathorpe, Wappenbury, Hunningham and Offchurch, and whilst small meanders diminish, its starts to perform larger ones. After a great loop near Offchurch the river runs parallel to the Grand Union Canal for a mile before diving into the centre of Royal Leamington Spa.

Leamington in its early 19th century pomp was a spa town. Salty underground springs feed baths in the Pump Room, where fifty thousand people a year get treatment for rheumatic ailments in a modern treatment centre. Brave visitors can taste the waters from a fountain in the Pump Room Annexe.

This is the first place on the Leam of any significance, and by now the river has itself become important. Its Grade C waters, particularly their volume, upgrade the Avon from Grade D (formerly E) to Grade C.

The town fetes the river with decorative stone bridges, handsome gardens and big parks. It flows through the gorgeously ornamental Jephson Gardens, named after Dr Henry Jephson who did much to promote the town as a spa. Beyond Parade, the Leam passes the Pump Room and under Adelaide Bridge. Throughout the town, the north bank of the river contains many fine Georgian, Regency and early Victorian houses, while to the south is a mile of public parks and sports grounds.

Public access to the river and the continuity of a splendid walk is broken for about half a mile, but resumes at the point where we left the Avon.

Leamington Spa to Stratford

Immediately downstream of the confluence of the Leam, the Avon flows under an aqueduct carrying the Grand Union Canal. This is an attractive stone, classical structure, but the 1930's concrete parapet is crass.

You can follow the Avon's north bank for another mile to War-wick, and through St Nicholas Park to St Nicholas Bridge. Here are pavilions, shelters, public loos, swings, slides, wooden castles, a boathouse, people lazing on benches, children eating ice cream and bright beds of flowers; and over the tree tops is one of the classic views of the most complete medieval castle in England.

Warwick Castle towers above the River Avon, sheer grey walls massively impregnable. Overlooking the river is Caesar's Tower and the Watergate Tower, between which is the impressive Minstrel Gallery above the Great Hall.

The first castle on the site would have been a simple Norman motte and bailey, with wooden buildings. The later stone towers, curtain walls and ranges of buildings had a chequered history but were much restored in the early 17th century. During the Civil War the castle withstood a siege of a fortnight and in 1645 held over three hundred troops. In 1978 the castle was sold to Madame Tussards who operate it as one of Britain's premier tourist attractions.

At the foot of the castle walls you can see the weed grown piers of the old town bridge. Beneath the Castle the Avon splits in two, forming a long island in the castle grounds. The outflow from a small lake called New Waters in Castle Park (formed by damming the Tach Brook) soon adds to the river.

The Avon swings slowly from side to side of a broad, fertile valley and in 2 miles reaches the village of Barford. Barford's bridge over the Avon is a complete contrast to the dignified and ornamental stone, classical bridges of Leamington and Warwick. This is a low five arched country bridge in a yellow tinted limestone with a grey sandstone parapet. There are many more like it downstream, but not all have such regular sized arches. The Avon here is wide, it has power, and the big meanders hint at what wet weather might make it. No wonder Barford bridge has relief culverts on the north bank, The village was the birthplace of Joseph Arch who founded the Agricultural Workers Union.

Two more great meanders take the Avon on to Wasperton, then to Hampton Lucy and Charlecote. The landscape now is level, but there are low and sometimes steep little hills nearby, often forming a long cliff showing one of the river's former courses. As the river nears Hampton Lucy the valley floor is about 2 miles wide but the Avon flows close to a sharp rise on the western side.

Hampton Lucy and Charlecote are just half a mile apart on opposite banks of the river. Once linked by a ford, a bridge now crosses the river by the restored and flour producing Charlecote Mill - well worth a visit.

From the Victorian cast iron road bridge, a track on the Hampton Lucy bank leads upstream to a path. From here you can see the middle Avon at its best and assess its condition. The river has dropped 9 metres in the 8 miles since the confluence of the Leam, an average fall of 1.1 metres per mile. This is low and ought to be slow, but the Avon is getting bigger and the weight of water keeps it moving fast.

Charlecote Mill by the Avon

Curious warning - bridge over the Avon at Stratford

Here the river winds through level fields between clay banks eight feet high. It has been split about half a mile upstream to serve the mill, so you are seeing only two thirds or three quarters of its flow. The water is fast and clear, skidding round little reed beds and shoals of sand and gravel inside each bend. It forms bright little rills, there is no dank smell as at Ashow and it looks the picture of a lowland English river in good health. Only some lingering flecks of foam and a few eddies of scum suggest anything else, and perhaps the bed and the water itself looks a little dead.

Beside the river path is a tiny timber frame, brick and thatch house, bandaged in tarpaulins and hopelessly bedraggled. The walls are tumbled, chimneys shattered, timbers sagging rotten and floors broken. From one chimney sprouts a battered and defiant TV ariel.

The lives of the two villages have been tied to the Lucy family of Charlecote since the 16th century. Many of the local houses were built from clay taken from Brick Kiln Field on the estate and the first village schools were provided by the family.

Charlecote Park is managed by National Trust, but has been home to the Lucy family since 1247. The present house was built in the 16th century and was later visited by Elizabeth I. Victorian style interiors were later added to the rooms to give the house a more romantic feel. The river flows through the park landscaped by Capability Brown and beside the house. There are large herds of red and fallow deer, allegedly poached by Shakespeare, and a flock of Jacob sheep introduced in 1756.

At Charlecote the Avon passes for the third time through the park-land of a great house but is probably too big to be domesticated and featured, so rolls on for five miles past Alveston to Stratford upon Avon. The valley floor is now very flat, but the small hills are still there and control the river's direction from a distance. So as the Avon loops north from Alvaston to get round a low summit, it meets a cliff at Hatton Rock which deflects it south until at Avoncliffe it is turned west into the town.

One can scarcely write about the River Avon without mentioning Shakespeare - so there, we have done. The connection attracts thousands of visitors from all over the world, modern secular pilgrims who buy fake relics from souvenir shops. Stratford has other interesting features, but apart from the riverfront we do not find it particularly attractive. Swans are especially associated with the river at the town centre, but you will find no more than on the horribly dirty River Tame at Tamworth. You will not find the Royal Shakespeare Theatre anywhere else, but why is such a centre of the arts so dull outside.

The Upper Avon was first made navigable in 1637 but fell into disrepair. We explained in an earlier section how in the 1970's it was restored. Boaters were overjoyed but the navigation affects the character of the river. The locks and weirs maintain long reaches at specific depths and engines stir in exhaust fumes, with some fuel and lubricating oil. There are no more shoals and shallows and rills, and the wildlife would probably have preferred the river in its quieter, derelict state.

In the 6 miles since Hampton Lucy the Avon has barely fallen at all, a mere 3 metres or so, a rate of .5 metres per mile. But the river rolls on from Stratford, over its first weir with the lock in the willows by the north bank, under a vast new road bridge and past the racecourse and another lock.

Next comes a magnificent steel girder bridge which once carried the Great Western Railway's main line to Cheltenham. Once The Cornishman roared over the Avon, but not since 1976. Six miles of the line to Long Marston have been turned into a cycling and walking route which combine with riverside paths to make circular walks.

Along the Stour

Just under a mile downstream the Avon is joined by the River Stour flowing in from the south-east. A mile or so further on is Milcote Manor, with enormous chimneys dating from 1564. There is dispute as to whether it was this house, or Milcote Hall near Clifford Chambers, which was burned by Cromwell in the Civil War.

Milcote Hall Farm and Clifford Chambers are actually on the Stour, a 21 one mile long river which rises to the south-east at Wigginton Heath, running off the northern outliers of the Cotswold Hills. The headwaters first flow west through Stourton near Cherington and on to Mitford Bridge. Here they merge with the Nethercote Brook, Knee Brook and Paddle Brook and head north. By Tidmington they form quite a substantial watercourse. Past Willington, the Stour aims for Barcheston, opposite where the Pig Brook joins from the west. Just downstream is Shipston on Stour, then Honington.

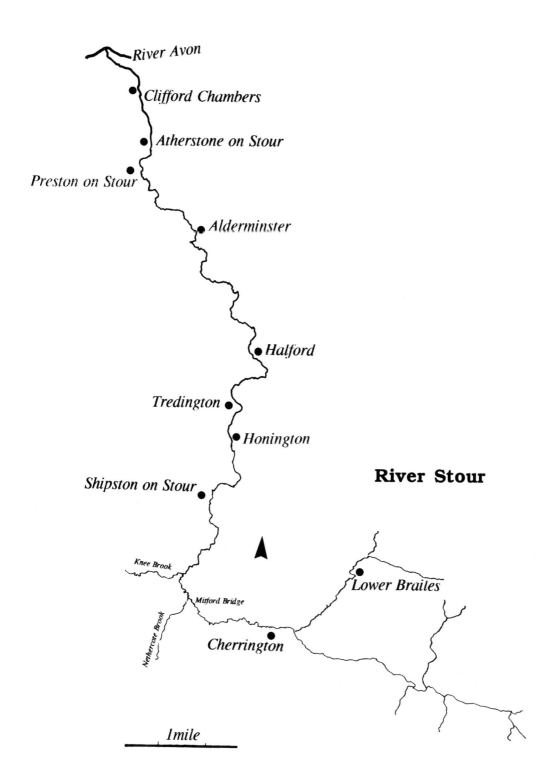

River Avon

Clifford Chambers

Atherstone on Stour

Preston on Stour

Alderminster

Halford

Tredington

Honington

River Stour

Shipston on Stour

Knee Brook

Mitford Bridge

Lower Brailes

Nethercote Brook

Cherrington

1 mile

Up to this point the river has run through a hilly landscape and been joined frequently by short, fast streams typical of the Cotswolds. Now the Stour is entering the flat and lazy country beside the Avon. It falls from its source at 190 metres by 118 metres in the 7.3 miles to Mitford bridge, a rate of 16 metres per mile. The next 13.5 miles includes a drop of 66 metres at 10.6 metres per mile to Halford, and in its last 8.5 miles it falls only about 17 metres or .5 metres per mile.

The next village of Tredington is close to the Roman Fosse Way, and its history goes back well before Domesday. The first recorded reference to it was in 757 when it was known as Tredincgtun. The landmark of the village is the parish church of St Gregory. The first church dates to 961 and both Saxon and Norman work can still be seen in the otherwise largely 14th century building. Look carefully at the fine oak door and you will see fragments of bullets said to have been left by the Roundheads. At neighbouring Halford a bridge carries the Fosse Way over the Stour.

Skirting Newbold on Stour, the river flows through Ettington Park. The Victorian house is now an hotel, but the park is still owned by the Shirleys, said to be the only family still holding land which they held at the time of the Norman Conquest.

Alderminster has grown over the past few years because it sits by the Stratford to Oxford road. The village church on the riverbank was founded by monks from Glastonbury and the oldest part of the village is grouped around it. It moved here from the top of the hill after 1348 when the Black Death wiped out much of the population. Another church stands alone in a field across the river.

These villages all sit right next to the river, quite unlike villages on many reaches of the Severn, Teme and Avon. Quite simply, the Stour is a small river and less to be feared. Its flow can grow considerably in winter but it is not handling the drainage from thousands of square miles and the variation is much smaller.

Next downstream is Wimpstone, then Preston on Stour. Unlike Alderminster, Preston has not suffered from new development because it was an estate village, part of the Alscot Estate. Downstream the river flows through Atherstone on Stour and Clifford Chambers. It has a single, wide street, at the far end of which Queen Anne style Milcote Manor hides behind high stone walls. Nearby is a water mill, now a house, which was the reason for two weirs.

The Stour flows on under the Stratford road into the Avon. Water quality is Grade A in the upper reaches and B from Mitford Bridge. This is a valuable contribution to the Avon and enables it to continue as Grade C.

The Stour to the Severn

As the Avon rolls on the valley floor becomes flat and sandy, with arable fields reaching out to distant small hills. It is not yet the vast plain of the Vale of Evesham, but this is a hint of what follows. For nearly ten miles until it has passed Welford, the river tends to hug the slightly higher land along its northern edge.

Less than a mile after the fresh waters of the Stour have improved the Avon, it takes the effluent from another sewage works, then about 2.5 miles downstream comes a third lock and weir at Luddington. There are thirteen to Tewkesbury and at each the river crashes over a weir, which has a valuable aerating effect on the water.

On the opposite bank is Luddington church in an unspoilt, black and white village approached along a tree lined avenue. The church was built in 1872 nearly one hundred years after the old one had burned down. Meanwhile, villagers were ferried across the river to Welford on Avon.

Just over a mile downstream is Weston on Avon, a pretty thatched village which is only a mile and a bit to Welford on Avon by road but 5 miles by river. The Avon has thrown a great loop to the north until pushed south again by Binton Hill. Since before Stratford there has been slightly higher ground to the north, but at Welford low hills from the south begin to close in as well. For the next few miles the contours become more interesting.

Only a mile beyond Welford the valley road climbs to what seems an immense height, but actually only 55 metres. Even so, looking down over the river and the valley 25 metres below the effect is impressive, perhaps more so because we have not previously seen such perspectives on the Avon.

The river flows on the 5.5 miles to Bidford on Avon, splitting to create an island at Bidford Manor and quite ignored by Barton, though there is a weir and lock. The land to the south is now becoming the sort of prosperous fruit and veg. country that will

The broad reach of the Avon downstream of Evesham

The comfortable hump of the old sandstone bridge at Pershore

soon claim the whole valley north from the foot of the Cotswold Hills.

Bidford on Avon is a fast growing small town with a pleasant core of older buildings but none of great historical interest. The main building is the 13th century Falcon Inn. The town was built on only one side of the river and comparison of the land levels will explain why. The bridge is a stone, medieval structure with arches of all sizes. It is narrow and the traffic is controlled by lights. The road follows the Roman Ryknild Street between Bourton on the Water on the Fosse Way, via Alcester and Birmingham to Watling Street.

Beyond Bidford, the Avon leaves Warwickshire for Worcester and the banks become deeper and steeper. A mile or so downstream from Bidford the river flows past Marlcliffe where its last main tributary the Arrow, joins from the north. You can walk the south bank from Bidford beyond Cleeve Prior and get good views of the confluence. Cleeve Prior ignores the Avon, which is a long way below, but here under a towering cliff is the biggest caravan site you can imagine, garnished with wooden chalets. Why so many acres and acres and all in white? The footpath continues to The Littletons where the brave can ford the river.

The Avon is heading into fruit growing country and orchards line the west bank as it swings south towards Evesham. With greenhouses, sheds and rows of caravans, the landscape has become dull and cultivated. The rest of the river's course is characterised by giant swings across a broad valley to skirt areas of slightly higher ground.

Evesham, like Shrewsbury, lies within a great loop of river, but its patch of higher ground is at only 40 metres with the river at about 22 metres. The remains of the 14th century Abbey sit by the riverside, which is popular for water sports. Pleasure craft can be hired and there is an annual regatta each Spring Bank Holiday.

The Avon approaches Evesham from the north and if it continued south-west it would head directly for the Severn. Why does it turn through a full circle before heading west? The contours in the gap between Evesham and the Severn. explain the reason. The foot of the Cotswold escarpment heads the river off a direct route south, and the apparent route around the southern side of Bredon Hill is at levels of 40 to 46 metres, against the river's 22 metres at Evesham. So this area is drained to the north and into the

Avon by the River Isbourne and some brooks. Over the summit near Aston under Hill, the Carrant Brook drains south-west into the Severn.

Not only does the Avon not run this way, but it once flowed north-east from Bredon Hill to the Trent. The change occurred when a huge ice sheet known as the Great Eastern thawed, dropping boulder clay between Nuneaton and Rugby and causing the river to run backward, south-west, into the Severn.

The Avon rolls west with a series of meanders on the 10 miles to Pershore. It is not generally accessible and the roads are at a distance, so it is difficult to see in this wide, level valley. However the character of the river remains much the same. On the way is Fladbury, a cluster of old houses, a pub and a church. On the opposite bank of the Avon is the mill, which you can reach on a hand operated ferry.

Pershore is a small market town around a great Abbey standing about half a mile from the river. The old six arched road bridge in pale yellow limestone has a brick parapet and a graceful hump. Its replacement is another 1920's concrete job with half hearted 18th century touches.

Here the Avon turns south-westerly, still swinging back and forth across its valley and as it leaves Pershore, running close under a wooded hillside. Indirectly but finally, it is running towards the Severn. To the west, the landscape is flat up to the Severn, and beyond for about 10 miles to the foot of the Malvern Hills. On the east side the big dome of Bredon pushes the Avon closer to the Severn.

The river still meanders, but these are the wide swings of a major river. All the more strange to find a single constriction at the Swan's Neck, where the loop is so tight that the Avon turns through 180 degrees within 100 metres. The bend is surrounded by gigantic arching willows. Further downstream, the landscape becomes ever flatter and the Avon wider and more regular; there are no more spectacular loops and it becomes rather dull.

The houses of Bredon are a delightful mixture of timber framing, brick and limestone, with roofs in tiles, slate and thatch. The National Trust have a tithebarn. However most of the buildings are a discreet distance from the Avon, which you can view from an area of grass and litterbins. It looks like a wide, fast moving canal.

To the west you can see the high embankment of the M5, and readers who use it in wet periods will know this area for a spectacular sheet of water lapping round Bredon on the far bank. However in normal weather the Avon is so controlled and regular as it passes under the M5 that it has little character.

The final reach of about 5 miles is straight, much of it from Bredon forming the Worcestershire and Gloucestershire boundary. In the historic town of Tewkesbury the Avon becomes interesting in a new way. Here is a marina and a lock, there are little urban bridges and people about their business. Just past the lock the river passes the flour mill and through the town to empty into the Severn.

Fladbury Mill on the Avon between Evesham and Pershore

River Arrow

The upper reaches

The River Arrow is one of the small rivers rising in the hills south of Birmingham and the Black Country. Others are the Black Country Stour, the Hoo Brook and the Salwarpe which flow to the Severn, and the Cole and Rea which join the Tame/Trent. The Arrow is the only one which joins the Avon, and it starts as a series of streams from the south-eastern sides of the Lickey Hills, Forehill and Wast Hill.

Some of these streams flow immediately into the Upper and Lower Bittell reservoirs, serving the Worcester & Birmingham Canal. They are important for birds and include a Site of Special Scientific Interest. The Arrow is little more than a well watered ditch as it curls tentatively round field edges to Alvechurch and past the site of a Bishop's Palace, with medieval moat and fish ponds.

On the way to Redditch there are further fish ponds on the west bank, and then the partially excavated remains of the Cistercian Bordesley Abbey, with yet more ponds. Here the Arrow receives water from the Dagnell Brook which swells it from a stream to a small river.

So far the Arrow has run just under 6 miles from the Upper Bittel Reservoir and fallen from 155 metres to 85, ie 75 metres, a rate of 12 metres per mile. This is no tumbling highland stream, but similar to the early stages of the Avon.

Redditch is a sprawling overspill town, or district, with a baffling system of roads and estates which all look alike. However there is a pleasant if undistinguished older core, and as all the old fish ponds and remains suggest, it has a long history. The key industries for many years have been needles and fishing tackle. This area is rather attractive, sheep graze the green spaces between estates and paths have been laid down to allow easy, year round walking.

The Arrow is here joined by streams from Rowney Green and Beoley in what is generally a wet area. It flows south through the district in a broad, green valley which has been very effectively planned as

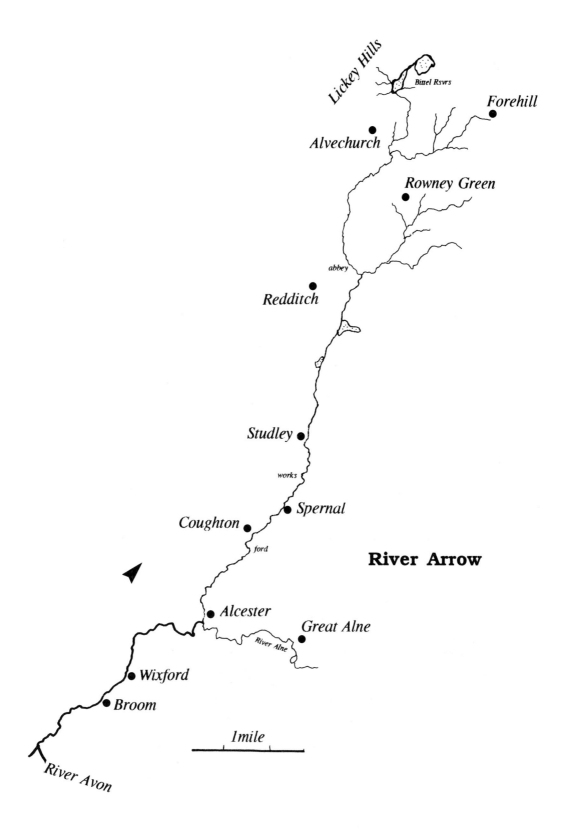

Lickey Hills

Bittel Rsvrs

Forehill

Alvechurch

Rowney Green

abbey

Redditch

Studley

works

Spernal

Coughton

ford

River Arrow

Alcester

Great Alne

River Alne

Wixford

Broom

1mile

River Avon

a public amenity. After a lake and several ponds, the Arrow emerges at Studley by another religious monument, a Priory.

Some 3.8 miles on from Alvechurch the river has fallen another 25 metres at a rate of 6.6 metres per mile. This is not the flow of a Team or Severn but makes the Arrow a brisk little river which, in spite of its small size, powered eight water mills and a forge. Water quality varies between Grades C and D.

Studley to Alcester

Studley is mentioned in Domesday but is a village with much modern building, almost all to the west of the river. Like Redditch, the main industry is needle making. Needles and fishing tackle used to be made in small factories tucked away behind the old buildings. In the 1930s these were largely consolidated into one company and Needle Industries' factory is now Britain's main producer.

The Arrow enters open countryside and winds through green fields between steep clay banks. The valley floor is level but there are interesting little "benches" marking previous changes of course. To the west is the long ridge on which the Romans built Ryknild Street between Bourton on the Water in the Cotswolds and Watling Street in Staffordshire. The motte of an old castle and the church lie to the east where the land rises into small hills.

Half a mile downstream the Arrow gets effluent from a sewage works serving Redditch and Studley, then flows on through flat fields past Spernal. Here is the most enormous old rectory, and a tiny church. It was deconsecrated in the 1930's and has been used as a sculptor's studio.

The river now starts to wind and twist between arable fields before arriving at Coughton. This attractive settlement was once at the edge of Feckenham Forest, and a cross marking the forest boundary stands opposite the post office. The most conspicuous feature is the elaborate Tudor gatehouse of Coughton Court, which was the seat of the Throckmortons since 1409. It is now in the care of the National Trust.

Beyond Coughton Court a lane fords the Arrow and a sign warns that the route is impassable when the river is in flood. The Arrow has travelled nearly 4 miles from Studley and fallen some 12 metres, a rate of 4 metres per mile. It has been joined by only a few small ditches and the sewage works but the water looks quite bright and clean.

Between Coughton and Alcester the river flows through more arable country, its course becomes even more tortuous and the banks often hold bits of rubbish. Perhaps it is the relatively slow current or a muddy bottom, but water quality now seems to decline. However the twists and bends do benefit wildlife by enclosing several small uncultivable patches of willows, alders and nettles, one of which has become a formal reserve.

Along the Alne

The centre of Alcester stands on the gravels of former river terraces and the River Arrow flows around three sides of the town before continuing south to the Avon.

Just east of the town centre the Arrow is joined by its only major tributary, the Alne. This modest river rises north-east of Redditch near Portway and only a few hundred yards from the River Blythe which flows north into the Tame and Trent.

The two arms of the infant Alne flow east to pass either side of Tanworth, head south-east to pick up a stream near Danzey Green, then south through Henley in Arden. It is nudged in this direction by the small and delightful hills between the Tanworth area and Alcester, Henley in Arden and Studley, in fact filling the triangle between the Arrow and the Alne. Towards the south they are called the Alne Hills, but the name could be applied to the whole block.

Through Henley the Alne is still very small, though in the past it has flooded the town. It creeps past the backs of the timber frame and brick buildings which line the main street, passes close by the remains of the castle and the Norman church, then disappears into fields towards Wootton Wawen.

Wootton Pool was made as an ornament to Wootton Hall where the Alne cascades over a weir. Joined by a smaller stream, it becomes a slightly larger river as it twists through pastoral farmland and past a small sewage works.

In its last 11 miles the Alne has an uneventful life. There is the site of a castle at Aston Cantlow, a big mill and weir at Great Alne (now apartments) and a medieval dovecote at Kinwarton (National Trust).

This is the archetypal lowland river of middle England, willows, bullrushes and placid, wandering reaches between low green banks. Water quality if the Alne varies between Grades C and D, having declined recently from largely Grade B status.

Alcester to the Avon

Alcester was a Roman town at the junction of Ryknild Street with the Saltway from Eatington through Alcester to Droitwich. Excavation has revealed roads, defences, buildings, burials, coin hoards and mosaic pavements. and there is evidence of Iron Age occupation.

Roman occupation of Britain was at first confined to the south-east of the rivers Trent, Avon and lower Severn. The Fosse Way was built just behind this early frontier and Alcester's close position made it an ideal place from which to expand the empire northwards.

Alcester is not mentioned in Domesday, but that does not mean the town did not exist at the time. There is a reference in the life of St Egwin, Bishop of Worcester written about 1100. Subsequently it became a prosperous market centre.

In the 2.75 miles south from Coughton the Arrow has fallen about 10 metres, a rate of 3.6 metres per mile, and therefore levelling from the previous rates of 4 and 6.5 metres. The Arrow is preparing to join the Avon in its huge, broad valley.

In fact the landscape south of Alcester does not immediately flatten out, rather the valley narrows and deepens for the next 1.5 miles between the dome of Oversley Hill to the east and Ragley Park in the west. But at Wixford the valley widens, funnel like, to become flat and willowy. Half a mile south at Broom are market gardens and level, fertile fields reaching away to Bidford and the Avon.

Wixford has a popular pub called the Fish, and the riverside path through the willows near the brick bridge bring to mind light summer rain and fishing gear. The next village of Broom has several timbered buildings and yet another mill, said to have been founded by the

Monks of Worcester. It used to be two mills under one roof and until a bridge was built about 1900, stood near a ford across the river. The Arrow was treacherous here after heavy rain and once a horse and cart were washed away.

The Arrow flows on for another two miles, collects the Ban Brook near Salford Bridge, passes a caravan site and Worcester Meadows to join the Avon downstream of Marlcliffe. In the 5.5 miles since Alcester the Arrow has fallen 11 metres, a rate of 2 metres per mile, indicating almost level and typical of a lowland river. It brings to the Avon a supply of Grade C water because of the output from four sewage works. Inland rivers cannot escape this role, we just have to learn how to do the thing well.

Wixford's graceful brick bridge. The Heart of England Way Long Distance Footpath passes by behind the camera.

River Trent

Introduction

The Trent is not the longest river in Britain but is probably the most important. Flowing in a giant U shaped course for 167 miles from Biddulph Moor to the Humber estuary, it has long formed the boundary between north and south. The Romans knew it as Trisantona, but by the 8th century it was called Treonte. From that it was a short step to Trent.

Compared with our other main rivers, Severn and Avon, the Trent is the least rural and its valley the broadest and flattest. Nearly six million people live within the Trent's catchment, mainly in the major towns and cities of the Midlands. They need vast amounts of power and lie in a region well supplied with coal. So the banks of the Trent has the largest concentration of power stations and cooling towers in the country.

The Trent is a prime coarse fishery with about 35 species present. Today's situation is similar to that before the Industrial Revolution although the intervening years saw a dramatic decline. Fish started to decline in the 19th century, largely due to pollution from the Potteries, Burton and the River Tame. Sturgeon were early sufferers. Another was the burbot, the only freshwater species of the cod family. At one time it was widespread and common, particularly in East Anglia. It disappeared from the Trent in the 1920s and has not been seen in Britain since the 1960s. Cleaner rivers may allow reintroduction from Europe. Meanwhile any burbot which may have escaped detection are now officially protected.

In the 19th century, the Trent was a major salmon fishery. In 1884 213 salmon rod licences were issued, catching 450 fish with an average per rod of 121 pounds. But the salmon suffered from industrialisation and obstructions such as weirs which hindered passage upstream. Recent years have seen salmon as far upstream as Castle Donington in Leicestershire and reintroduction may be viable. The principal species in the river today are roach, chub, dace, bream, silver bream, pike, carp and gudgeon. Barbel were absent as recently as the 1960s but are returning vigorously.

*Up the Trent - Essex Bridge
at Shugborough*

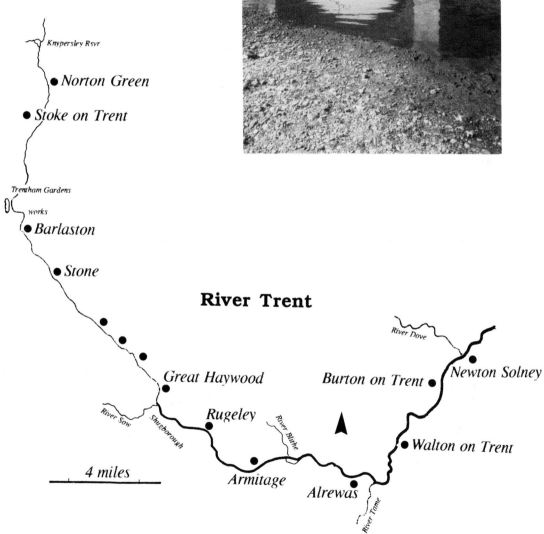

Knypersley Rsvr

● *Norton Green*

● *Stoke on Trent*

Trentham Gardens

works

● *Barlaston*

● *Stone*

River Trent

River Dove

● *Newton Solney*

Burton on Trent ●

● *Great Haywood*

River Sow

Shugborough

Rugeley

River Blithe

● *Walton on Trent*

4 miles

● *Armitage*

Alrewas ●

River Tame

Source to Tittensor

The River Trent rises at around 280m above sea level on Biddulph Moor, between Biddulph and Leek. The main stream rises on the Millstone Grit close to the Peak District. It soon passes through Knypersley Reservoir and Greenway Bank Country Park, before reaching the Productive Coal Measures and the north-eastern outskirts of Stoke on Trent.

In this first 5 miles the river falls 145 metres, a rate of 29 metres per mile, the steepest being 38 metres per mile in the first 1.8 miles. For a major river the Trent has a short upland section. As you might expect, this is also its cleanest section, but the Trent starts as Grade C, improves to Grade B from the Reservoir but crashes to Grade D for a mile or so as it enters Stoke.

The Trent sneaks unnoticed through the city, thought about no more than a drain, which is what it is. Water quality does recover briefly to Grade C as it leaves town and passes through Trentham Gardens. Through the parkland and under the A34 it is still a small river, rather sullen and dead looking, then 300 yards on it meets the massive Strongford Water Treatment Works.

The works covers acres with settlement tanks, filter beds, digestion tanks and all manner of exciting apparatus. It has improved water quality, and under the classification system in use until 1994 this was evident on the NRA's coloured maps. However under the new system the Trent falls to Grade D for the half mile to Tittensor, then recovers to Grade C as far as Stone. At Tittensor it has fallen another 30 metres at a rate of only 4 metres per mile.

Tittensor to Shugborough

The valley floor is only about a mile wide as the Trent turns south. There are low hills to the west as the river flows into Keuper Marl country around Tittensor Chase and the wooded Iron Age hillfort of Bury Bank, Darlaston. For centuries this valley has been a major transport corridor. The A34 is the historic route from London to the north-west and Scotland, and here the A51 branches north-west, the medieval road from London to Chester and Ireland. On the east side of the valley is the railway from Stoke with lines of pylons.

Less than a mile south of the Strongford plant you can assess its work from the Barlaston road bridge. The water is visibly cleaner and has some sparkle, yet the bed is still sludge brown. After the disused Meaford Power Station the valley narrows and the river snakes back and forth across it in amazing contortions. At Stone the Trent has travelled another four miles but fallen only 8 metres, at 2 metres per mile.

Here the river is joined by the innocent looking Scotch Brook. Its source is three miles north-east at Barlaston Common, from where it flows through a deep, rocky valley to Stone. It passes Mosty Lea Mill which is now being restored by Stafford Borough Council as a tourist attraction. At the bottom of Stone High Street the Brook is culverted beneath a car park, but from time to time breaks out. During a storm a few years ago the quantity and force of the flood washed away the road and flooded the town.

Near the confluence of the Scotch brook the Trent has become narrower and faster and a canoe course has been developed on the raging "white waters", though it does seem a bit tame. You can see it from Stone's main bridge, a modern concrete affair. Beside it is a stout, old, grey sandstone bridge with three arches, now retired.

South of Stone the landscape is softer and greener with less visible industry. The Trent continues its looping habit through the hamlet of Aston by Stone, where the moated hall is a home for retired priests. A brick bridge carries the lane over the Trent and the banks are clustered with wild flowers. The Trent & Mersey Canal is very close and follows the river. The valley floor is only .75 miles wide and the sides are sudden and steep as the result of two big and nearly parallel geological faults.

The small hamlet of Burston is just off the main road and clusters round a pond by the river and canal. By contrast Sandon is an estate village right on the main road, an example of a place whose location was decided by the lord of the manor. Once there were two villages. Great Sandon was on the hill near the now isolated church, the present village on the coach road was called Little Sandon, and Sandon Hall was tucked away on a moated island. When the lord decided to empark his estate he felt that Great Sandon spoiled the view, so had it obliterated. The Hall was later burned down.

Sandon's main bridge has a mellow sandstone parapet, but underneath is a typical 1949 concrete job. The river is deep and fast, but looks brown and slightly unhealthy with flecks of foam.

Rampant wild plants at Aston by Stone

White water (!) canoeing starts here by Stones's old bridge

From the river in Salt village you can see the Pitt Column in Sandon Park, in memory of the Prime Minister Sir Robert Peel who had many connections with Staffordshire. By the War Memorial and opposite the Dog and Doublet is the headquarters of the Staffordshire Wildlife Trust. If you want to do something positive to protect the local countryside, drop in and join.

This stretch of the Trent Valley between Burston and Weston floods regularly. There still remain some wet meadows which are important for breeding wading birds like redshank, lapwing and snipe. Few of them have escaped ploughing and re-seeding so they do not support the range of wild flowers that they might.

On 19th March 1643 the battle of Hopton Heath was fought on the hill above Salt, the only major one of the English Civil Wars to be fought in Staffordshire. Sir John Gell and Sir William Brereton were on the Parliamentary side and agreed to try and occupy Stafford. Advance troops which entered Great Haywood on the 17th were flushed out by Royalists who knew of Gell's movements. Realising the enemy already controlled Stafford, the battle took place at Hopton. The Parliamentary forces were defeated, although the Royalist commander, the Earl of Northampton, was killed. The dead of both sides were buried at Sandon and Weston churches. Today the "heath" is a wooded hillside crossed by footpaths but now and then canon balls and musket shot turn up in the local fields.

At Weston the valley floor is some 2 miles wide where the Gayton Brook joins the Trent. This attractive little stream fords the road at the edge of Gayton village. It contains the combined waters of a handful of small streams which drain the hilly country around Milwich. The village pub is the Saracen's Head and the sign shows a Saracen and a Christian smirking over an improper joke.

The name Salt is a mystery. The village has held it since before Domesday but there is no evidence that salt was ever produced. It may once have been a market place for salt produced in Stafford and at Shirleywich three miles to the south-east. Salt is certainly present all around here and several salt springs reach the surface.

One such spring bubbles up at Pasturefields near Shirleywich, where the Staffordshire Wildlife Trust have a riverside nature reserve. The saline water encourages plants which normally live on the coast, such as sea plantain, common saltmarsh grass, lesser sea spurrey, saltmarsh rush and sea arrowgrass. To maintain this range of species the reserve has to be grazed by cattle, and because of the threat of trampling the plants or disturbing nesting snipe, redshank and lapwing, visitors must first get permission from the Trust. This is a reserve for the specialist and to most people it will look little different from the surrounding flat fields.

The 9 miles of the Trent Valley south from Stone have been broad with sweeping green pastures. In this distance the river has fallen only some 10 metres, a rate of .7 metres per mile, and this is reflected in its meandering course.

Near Great Haywood the Trent passes over a small weir. Upstream it is a sullen brown with a dank, dead smell, but the tumble over the rocks helps to oxygenate the water and improve its appearance. The effect is temporary, for downstream the river returns to a regular channel, smooth and deep with unpleasant secrets.

Between the village of Great Haywood and Shugborough Park the Trent is joined by the River Sow, and nearby the Trent & Mersey Canal is joined by the Staffordshire & Worcestershire Canal.

Great Haywood is a pleasant riverside village, but due to the boundaries of the Park it virtually ignores the setting and turns its back on the river. It is linked to Shugborough by the pedestrian Essex Bridge, a spectacular fourteen arch sandstone structure only four feet wide. It is often described as a packhorse bridge, but was built in the late 16th century by the Earl of Essex for huntsmen, horses and dogs on their way from his home at Chartley Hall to Cannock Chase.

Shugborough Park is the home of the Earl of Lichfield but owned by the National Trust and managed by Staffordshire County Council. The park has a collection of dotty follies and a farm museum with rare breeds. The Hall is open to the public and the buildings also house the County Museum.

The land around Essex Bridge where the Sow meets the Trent and the Trent & Mersey Canal passes by is used for walks, picnics, dog strolling, stone skimming and lolling around. The water quality of the Trent at this point is only Grade D, but still the children paddle and try to splash Grandad and Auntie Brenda. However the Sow makes a visible improvement to Grade C which lasts for some 18 miles to the confluence of the River Tame.

Essex Bridge hops over the Trent at Great Haywood

High Bridge near Handsacre. The picture was taken after the book was written and shows the old bridge being replaced.

Rugeley's river bridge is unseen and neglected. This handsome, grey sandstone arch is discreetly classical, except for the four jolly ornamental lamp standards with barley sugar stems and small curly brackets. They are out of use and deteriorating but should be preserved.

The Trent briefly returns to the canalside near Armitage. In 7.6 miles from Wolseley Bridge it has fallen only 3 metres, about .4 metres per mile, or virtually flat. Close by is an environmental study centre for school children within the grounds of the power station. They learn about the wildlife which has colonised an old gravel pit left when gravel to build the station was extracted. It is a surprisingly varied site with a host of waterfowl, wild flowers and insects, some having been helped to colonise by judicious planting.

On the north side of the river from Armitage is the hamlet of Mavesyn Ridware. By the river in 1403 Sir Robert Mavesyn fought and killed his neighbour Sir William Handsacre, when they rode out to join opposite sides in the battle of Shrewsbury. Mavesyn went on to the battle, supporting Henry IV against Harry Hotspur and Owen Glendower, and although the King won the battle, Mavesyn was killed. The name is a contraction of malvoisins, meaning dangerous neighbours.

The Trent now becomes broad and majestic, a major river requiring large bridges. High Bridge was built at Coalbrookdale in the Severn valley in 1830. It is out of use and obscured by a Bailey Bridge placed to carry traffic, but you can see it from the east side. The single cast iron arch is heavily braced and stands on hexagonal columns with massive, stumpy sandstone abutments. It is obviously corroded beyond repair and supported by modern girders.

From Shugborough the Trent flowed a fairly straight course in a valley narrowed by Cannock Chase on one side and low hills on the other. But at Handsacre it broadens into a plain which soon becomes miles wide. At Kings Bromley some 6 miles from Armitage, the river has fallen only another 4 metres, continuing the gentle .4 metres per mile which has not varied much in the 11.5 miles from Rugeley.

The Trent is a now a big and powerful river, so it is surprising that there are records of this stretch drying up in the past. The first record of 1110 is in Plot's "Natural History of Staffordshire". The other occasion on 21st December 1581 is noted in the Alrewas parish register. Were winters drier then than they have recently been?

Power stations & pastures

Beyond Shugborough, the river flows through water meadows.
On the north side of the valley is the Trent & Mersey Canal, the
railway line from Stoke on Trent follows it and is joined from the
west by the main West Coast line between London and Scotland.
On the south side is the brown and green flank of Cannock Chase.

Almost a mile on, the Trent passes under an austere road bridge of
Staffordshire blue brick. This is Weetman's Bridge, named after the
man who paid for it in 1888 when it replaced a perilous 200 foot
timber span. In total contrast is elegant Wolseley Bridge with its
three leaping sandstone arches of classical design. The view of the
bridge is now spoilt by the enormous pyramidal roof of a garden
centre, part of Wolseley Garden Park. This newly landscaped garden
in the grounds of the demolished Wolseley Hall has a wild flower
meadow and collection of willows and is a good place to see kingfishers on the river. Crassly, some wild flower rich water meadows
were destroyed to create it.

Close to Wolseley Bridge the Stafford Brook joins the river from
Cannock Chase. At this stage, some 2.75 miles from the confluence
of the Sow the river has fallen another 11 metres, so the rate of fall
has now increased to 4 metres per mile, compared with the previous
7 metres

The Trent both looks and smells better as it rolls on, and for a
mile or so the riverside becomes more rural. Just before the scene
is shattered by Rugeley and its power stations, the Trent & Mersey
Canal crosses the river on an aqueduct to pass south-east of the
power stations. The Trent passes east of the town picking up the
Bourn Brook, a 7 mile long tributary from the north. It passes
through Lount Farm, where the owner continues to farm in a traditional way to the benefit of his flower filled meadows. Joining
from the west and draining the main east-west valley dividing
Cannock Chase is the Rising Brook.

Water quality remains at Grade C but the Trent has received the
waters of several little brooks since Shugborough, three of them
bringing good quality water off Cannock Chase. These constant
small contributions help the Trent maintain its quality in spite
of passing Rugeley and other towns.

Before King's Bromley, the Trent splits in two. The northern branch is joined by the River Blithe, a particularly fine river with good, clean stretches which brings good Grade C water.

The southern branch of the river passes close to the village and a large gravel pit. At Manor Farm, CHADS, an organisation concerned with both disabled people and conservation, has developed a nature reserve with disabled access. Nearby they are working on another ambitious project to restore some riverside land to water meadows and encourage the return of wild flowers and waders.

The two branches of the river rejoin before meandering on through the immense flatness of its valley past 17th century Orgreave Hall. Only the low plateau of the Needwood Forest to the north shows as a prominent ridge. A mile or so on the River Swarbourn flows in at the start of a very watery few miles. This is 4 miles downstream of Kings Bromley and the river has fallen another 4 metres. This rate of 1 metre per mile compares with the .4 metres to Kings Bromley

Along the Swarbourn

The Swarbourn is called a river, but at some 12 miles long is more an interesting stream. Its headwaters are the Eland Brook and Mare Brook which rise a couple of miles apart on the northern edge of the south tilted Needwood plateau.

The Eland Brook is the more northerly of the two and passes through a private lake at Holly Bush before continuing to Newborough. This small village never grew into the town hoped for by its 13th century founder, Robert Ferrers, Earl of Derby. Here the waters are blessed each May in one of two well dressing ceremonies in Staffordshire.

From Newborough the brook runs south through a quiet valley to Hoar Cross, where it is joined by the Mare Brook which has flowed through another little valley past the woods at Jackson's Bank. At Far Hoar cross, the combined waters have become the River Swarbourn and form a big ford across a minor road.

South through Woodmill and Woodlane, the next place is Yoxall, thought to have been a Celtic settlement with a Romano British burial ground. The river runs along the eastern edge of the village and is crossed by five bridges. For a pleasant riverside walk, take the footpath south off the Barton road, just east of the main road junction in the village. Continue beyond the houses along a track and take the second footpath left. There is a good chance of spotting a barn owl. At a small lane turn right, cross the river bridge, then turn right along the bank. As you walk back towards Yoxall watch for spring and summer wildflowers. You are unlikely to see the freshwater crayfish as they are nocturnal, but they are certainly there.

From Yoxall the Swarbourn continues through the fields around Wychnor to Alrewas - the name means the alder marsh, a very apt name for this village in wet ground. It has long been an important place beside the Roman Ryknild Street, now the A38.

From the limited information we have on the quality of the Swarbourn, which passes through arable farmland, we would expect it to be Grade C. It falls from 135 metres to 55 in 12 miles, a drop of 80 metres at 6.6 metres to the mile.

Alrewas to Burton upon Trent

The Trent & Mersey Canal passes through the centre of Alrewas, and just north of the village river and canal merge for 200 yards. The Trent enters over a broad weir crossed by a long footbridge which is easily reached from the village. When they separate the canal runs north and the river heads towards the gravel pits of Alrewas and Croxall.

St. Leonard's Church and the area around Wychnor are delightful, if you do not mind the gravel pits beyond the A38. The church dates mainly from around 1300, and the hummocky ground nearby was the site of an Anglo Saxon settlement deserted in medieval times. Through the Countryside Stewardship scheme there is access to the site and the landowner receives payments to maintain this historic landscape.

The quality of the Trent was maintained at Grade C by the Blithe, and the Swarbourne brings further clean water. Just under a mile south of the A38 the River Tame joins the Trent, bringing Grade E water. However within 350 yards the Trent is also swollen by the River Mease from south Derbyshire and Leicestershire which is decidedly cleaner. We have limited data on the Mease, but in its fourteen or so miles it only passes a couple of villages. This is arable country so we would expect it to be no worse than Grade

C. At all events, the result for the Trent is that it falls to Grade D for just a short stretch before recovering to Grade C, which it maintains past Burton on Trent and out of our area.

The Trent now turns north-eastwards, in places forming the boundary between Staffordshire and Derbyshire. Beyond Catton Hall on the east bank, the river again splits in two before the channels re-unite at Fatholme near Walton on Trent. The 1990s have seen some controversy here over the use of jet skis on the river.

Beyond Walton the landscape is dominated by the elevators and pyramid heaps of gravel pits, the chimneys and pink cooling towers of power stations and vast stalking pylons. It is very, very flat and the only hint of higher ground is the smudge of Cannock Chase to the north-east and the scarp of the Needwood Plateau to the north. To the south there are a few low hills with small blocks of woodland.

The gravel pits are in various stages of exploitation with some active, some recently abandoned and others already colonised by wildlife. At Branston is a water park run by East Staffordshire Borough Council where walking, fishing, wind surfing, picnicing, kite flying and sibling splashing are combined with a Staffordshire Wildlife Trust nature reserve. On the Derbyshire bank is the massive Drakelow Power Station complex. Gravel pits were dug to supply materials for the station and have flooded to form a wildfowl reserve. Access is by permit only from Powergen, but there is a good range of water birds and several hides.

The Drakelow and Branston wetlands have a wide range of bird life with large numbers of Canada geese which move regularly between various lakes. There are mallard, tufted duck, coot, moorhen, mute swan and great crested grebe. Cormorants are frequent and, in winter pochard and goldeneye. A number of waders come, including a few oystercatchers. The reed bed at Branston Water Park is one of the largest in Staffordshire and in summer is popular with reed and sedge warblers.

Water used for cooling the Trent's power stations is returned to the river at a higher than normal temperature. This so called thermal pollution can be a serious problem leading to fish deaths, although they are now rare.

The river is wide and fast and deep as it enters the series of broad meadows through the centre of Burton upon Trent known as The Washlands. In the 10.75 miles since the confluence of the Swarbourne it has fallen 8 metres, a rate of .75 metres per mile and a slight

*The Trent flows from under the long
bridge to join the canal at Alrewas.*

Stone skimming at Ferry Bridge, Burton on Trent.

levelling from the previous 4 miles. The Trent is now a very big river and floods regularly in winter. Flood defences between Sandon and Burton since 1937 have greatly reduced the threat. Floods on the scale that inundated Burton in 1947 no longer happen, although the Washlands are often a moving sheet of brown water.

People have said that Burton is best viewed from the A38, quickly. We think this is jolly unfair, and not just because John Drewett lived here for a few years. We can talk about the beer in a minute, but there are few towns with such a spectacular centrepiece as The Washlands. Whether you prefer the swans gliding on the river, the meadows of wild flowers, the trim trail for keep fit enthusiasts, the multicoloured splendour of Stapenhill Gardens or you are only here for the beer, this is a town to enjoy from the riverside. To get the full experience, try one of the trip boats. (Yes, yes - the breweries do have visitor centres but we don't know if they give free samples.)

Burton has three main bridges and there is little to say about the modern St Peter's Bridge. Burton Bridge, once called Trent Bridge, dates from the twelfth century but probably replaced a predecessor. The present sandstone bridge is 400 yards long in a simple classical style with so many arches it is almost a viaduct. The original structure took a slightly different line from today's bridge and was strategically crucial. Several battles were fought for it, notably in 1322 and during the 17th century English Civil Wars. By the mid 19th century increased traffic had made the bridge into a serious bottleneck. It was described as having *"the threefold distinction of being the longest, the most ancient and the most inconvenient structure of its kind in the United Kingdom"*. The Midland Railway Company got permission to erect the present bridge in 1859 and the old one was demolished in 1876.

The other bridge is Ferry Bridge, an exuberant cast iron suspension footbridge painted black and white. The raised cast iron walk across the whole of the Washlands links Burton to the suburb of Stapenhill and allows pedestrians and cyclists to cross the meadows in all weathers. Before it was opened in 1899 part of the journey was made by crossing the Old Fleet Stones, which was impossible during flooding.

Brewing was first developed by the monks of the 11th century Burton Abbey. In the 18th century Burton beer was shipped down the Trent as far as Poland and Russia. Today brewery buildings and silos dominate the town, and the river is overlooked by the red brick Bass water tower. The breweries use enormous quantities of water, but not the Grade C stuff from the Trent. The secret of the beer lies in the hard water pumped from underground springs. The underlying rocks contain gypsum and the water dissolves salts such as magnesium and calcium sulphates which help to give the beer its taste. The water is so important that in the past, brewers from other parts of the country have sunk wells in the area and carted it home.

The various channels of the Trent merge in the northern part of the town before flowing past the Clay Mills Water Treatment Works, where an old gravel pit plays a part in the treatment process. The pit is an excellent place for bird life and one tree has for long been a major cormorant roost.

A mile from Burton Bridge the Trent leaves Staffordshire for the last time, and opposite the pretty village of Newton Solney is the confluence with the River Dove. The rivers make a vast, glassy spread of water, sprawling over green fields between low banks. It looks lovely, but smells flat and stale just above the confluence where it is Grade C. However Grade B water from the Dove brings improvement, and with Grade B help from the Derwent the Trent maintains this standard for many miles.

The valley floor narrowed as the river approached Burton, and from Stapenhill there are attractive cliffs on the south side, the north-western edge of the Mease Uplands. At the confluence the land up the Dove Valley to the north is, once more, pancake flat. In the 2.5 miles from Burton Bridge the river has fallen about 4 metres, or 1.5 metres per mile, twice the fall before Burton.

There are a couple of miles between the river and A38 here and the land is a pleasant mosaic of flat green fields, pools, streams and ditches, all fringed with old willows.

To the sea

With Burton behind, the Trent heads out of this region on its long journey to the sea. Past Willington power station where peregrine falcons now nest in a specially built box, the river reaches Swarkestone. There has been a causeway here across the wet meadows of the Trent since the 13th century, and it marks the most southerly point reached by Bonnie Prince Charlie's army in 1745.

Downstream is Shardlow, once a major inland port on the Trent & Mersey canal and now supporting a large marina. Further still and the Trent reaches Nottingham, capital of the East Midlands, where its broad width is bordered by tree lined boulevards and crossed by the famous Trent bridge.

Flowing through Newark on Trent below the impressive castle ruins, it turns north, at last aiming purposefully towards the sea. By Gainsborough it has left behind all traces of hilly countryside and become a very big river with crossing points only at the M180 and A18 near Scunthorpe. The Trent reaches the Humber at Blacktoft Sands, a reserve of the Royal Society for the Protection of Birds where avocets now breed.

Burton Mill on an autumnal river

River Sow

A vital link

The River Sow is 21 miles long and rises near the Shropshire border 5 miles east of Market Drayton. It flows south-east across Staffordshire to join the Trent at Shugborough, and though it is nowhere deep or wide, it is very important indeed for wildlife.

The source is only .4 mile east of the headwaters of the Coal Brook, which flows west into the River Tern and the Severn. It therefore forms a link between the Trent and Severn river systems, making it an ideal route for migrating water birds. Because they need wet places at which to feed they tend to follow rivers, and the Sow is part of their route between the east coast and Wales.

The Sow is also likely to help otters recolonise Staffordshire. These delightful and popular mammals declined so much in the 1950s and 1960s that they were almost extinct in the county. But in the 1980s and 1990s otters have spread from Wales across Shropshire. One or two have found their way into Staffordshire, but most of the evidence for their presence comes from sites in the extreme west. If their present expansion continues, a clean river like the Sow reaching out to these border regions could provide conditions to encourage them to come east.

The Sow is clean despite the effluent from Brancote sewage works at Stafford, and delivers good Grade C water to the Trent. Above the confluence of its main tributary the Penk, about 4.25 miles from the Trent, it has long been of good standard. However the Penk was polluted by storm water and the effluent from Cannock Sewage Works. Improvements there have raised the quality of the Penk and this final section of the Sow.

Early stages

The source of the Sow at 190 metres is in a landscape of small green hills, and it first runs south-east round the south-west flank of a block of higher ground. Nearby is the magnificent black and white timbered Broughton Hall, between Eccleshall and Market Drayton.

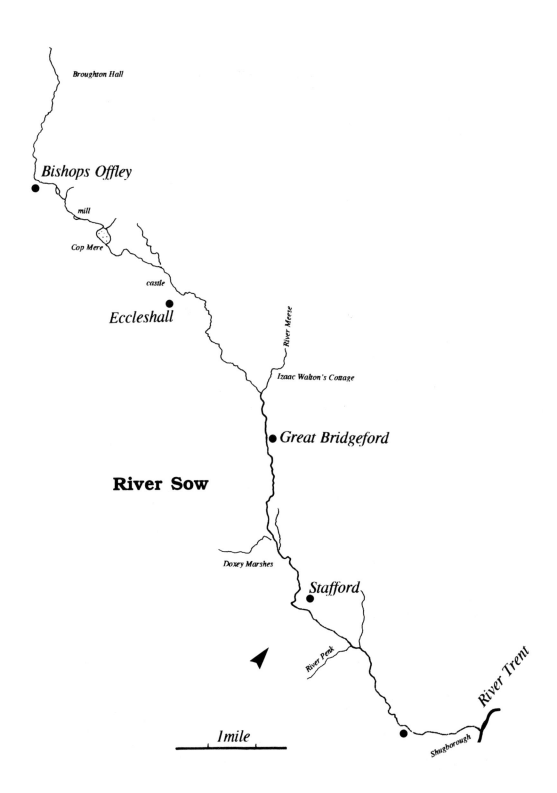

Broughton Hall

Bishops Offley

mill

Cop Mere

castle

Eccleshall

River Meese

Izaac Walton's Cottage

● *Great Bridgeford*

River Sow

Doxey Marshes

Stafford

River Penk

River Trent

Shugborough

1mile

The original building dates from the 13th century but was extensively remodelled in 1637. From the 18th century it became less important to the family and deteriorated until sold and restored in 1914.

The Sow heads south on the eastern edge of the massive Bishop's Wood. Today it is mainly conifers but was once part of a big oak forest, the ancient Blore Park covering 1800 acres. Some of the trees provided timber for Broughton Hall. Excavations during the 1920's revealed the remains of an Elizabethan glass furnace which is now preserved deep in the wood.

Throughout this stretch of the Langot valley the river follows a lane, until close to Outlands. One resident, William Wakeley, is buried a few miles away at Adbaston, where an inscription over the church porch reads:

Near this place lieth the body of William Wakely, late of the Outlands, in this parish, who died November 28th 1714 aged 125 years.

Now the river swings east past a string of settlements sharing the name Offley, derived from Offa's Leah meaning woodland cleared by Offa. Whether this is the Offa of the dyke, a relative or some-one else is not known. The Sow flows between Bishop's Offley to the south and Offleybrook to the north, powering a mill which still grinds corn.

Approaching the mill, the Sow runs through a marsh which is a reserve of Staffordshire Wildlife Trust. This is a delightful place in summer when it is alive with flowers and insects, including a range of dragonflies. You must get permission to visit.

Just downstream, the next mill pond served Walk Mill. This was recorded in Domesday and named because it was used for fulling woollen cloth. Here it was pounded to squeeze out excess grease, originally by putting it in a tray of water and stamping (walking) on it. The process was mechanised by water wheels driving shafts to pound the cloth with heavy blocks. Walk Mill was eventually converted to a corn mill but was badly damaged by a gale in 1976.

Less than a mile downstream is Cop Mere. Covering nearly fifty acres, it is the only Staffordshire mere to have a through flow of water. The Bishop of Lichfield held the fishing rights, but a deed has been traced which grants the lord of the manor of Charnes the right of *"fishing once a year in Copmere Pool as far as a man could throw a twopenny hatchet"*. Whatever that was, in the 4.8 miles from its source the Sow has fallen through 95 metres to 85 metres, a rate of nearly 20 metres to the mile. That however, is the end of its career as an upland stream.

On to Eccleshall

The Sow flows past Pershall, where there are a number of Jacobean buildings, then around the north side of Eccleshall Castle. This stretch was considerably deepened in the 1970s, until when a branch stream flowed through Castle Mere. The mere, which is a Staffordshire Wildlife Trust reserve, has silted badly since then and is little more than a large reed bed. Even so it supports a small but growing heronry.

To the north a mass of small streams drains the low land at the confluence of the Brockton Brook. It seems to have an intoxicating effect on the Sow which looses all direction as it coils and loops into a broad valley, in fact the eastern edge of the Trent Valley.

Some time before the Norman conquest the King gave a large area of land at Eccleshall to the Bishops of Lichfield. Placed midway between the two centres of the diocese - Lichfield and Chester, it was ideal for a residence, and remained the Bishops seat until the late 19th century.

Permission to fortify the Castle was given in 1200 but work was not completed until the early 14th century. Staffordshire largely fell to the Parliamentarians in the Civil War and by June 1643, the Royalist Bishop's castle was under siege. It was well defended, with corner towers, a moat and a large mill pond, later described as the second largest stretch of water in Staffordshire. The Royalists held out for eight weeks but the castle was taken on 30th August. In 1646 it was partially demolished.

Between 1690 and 1695 Bishop Lloyd built a large country house on the site of the medieval building - the Eccleshall Castle of today. Bishops continued to live here until 1867, when they moved to Lichfield.

Izaak Walton

From Eccleshall the River Sow wriggles south-east through level farmland to be joined from the north by the Meece Brook. A mile upstream at Shallowford the Brook passes the cottage of Izaak Walton, author of *The Compleat Angler*. He was born in Eastgate Street, Stafford in 1593 but spent the later years of his life at Shallowford.

The cottage is now a museum, dedicated to Izaak and fishing. After many years with a tiled roof it was recently thatched and must look much as it did in Izaak's day. We can ignore the gantries of the main West Coast railway behind, but it was the sparks from steam trains which in 1939 prompted Stafford Corporation to tile the cottage.

Walton was the author of several biographies, but it was *The Compleat Angler* which made him most famous. It was first published in 1653, shortly before he bought the cottage. Although he must have fished local rivers he is most associated with the waters of Dovedale.

Mills & marshes to Stafford

At the Meece Brook confluence the Sow has travelled 5.7 miles from Cop Mere and fallen only 2 metres, a rate of .2 metres per mile. This minimal fall explains the river's extraordinary contortions. The fall now increases but the contortions continue.

Downstream is Worston Mill, now a restaurant with grounds by the river. A nature trail has been laid out with information signs and observation points from which to watch wildlife. The current mill building dates from 1814 but the site has been used for milling since 1279. At first it chopped and ground wood, but for a period during the nineteenth century became a silk mill. Like Walton's cottage, it suffered from the trains because vibrations broke the silk threads. In 1932 it became a corn mill and survived as such until 1970.

Beyond Great Bridgeford the Sow loops back on itself several times in the soft ground, and in time might cut off the loops to form ox bow lakes.

Near Cresswell are the ruins of a chapel on the site of a deserted
medieval village. The Domesday survey recorded a water mill. The
chapel was built around 1200, but was destroyed in the 16th century,
by which time the main remnant of the village was the Manor House.
There are still a few humps and bumps in the fields. A bridlepath
to Seighford crosses the river by a footbridge.

The Sow and the almost parallel Darling Brook continue below the
massive viaduct of the M6. Motorway builders do not go along with
untidy rivers that wander about. For .8 of a mile the Sow runs an
obedient and miserable straight line to the Doxey Marshes. The
engineers would probably tell us that they had to safeguard the
viaduct in soft, watery ground, but we wonder whether strict toilet
training may have been a factor.

Doxey Marshes just over a mile north-west of Stafford is one of the
most important nature reserves in the County. The 360 acres of open
land managed by the Staffordshire Wildlife Trust are a particularly
valuable wildlife refuge, being surrounded on three sides by the
suburbs of Stafford and on the other by the motorway.

Development of the wetlands can be traced back to the 12th century
when a mill was built in Stafford, but the large areas of water seen
today did not really develop until the 20th century. Their origin
lies in the extraction of salt underlying much of this area by wild
brine pumping. Water is pumped into the soil to dissolve the salt,
then the solution is pumped out and the water evaporated. But this
leaves vast underground caverns which are liable to collapse. In
Stafford it became a serious problem leading to subsidence of roads
and buildings, until 1970 when pumping was stopped by court order.

The Wildlife Trust has put great effort into encouraging more
wildlife, creating a shallow scrape to attract birds which can be
watched from a hide. Meanwhile the flooded subsidence hollows
continue to grow. There are many waders including redshank and
oystercatcher, but the speciality of the marshes is a secretive brown
wading bird, the snipe. Living here all the year round, up to forty
pairs may be present. For much of the time the snipe remain hidden
in the reeds and grass, probing their long straight beaks into the
soft mud for food. Occasionally they pass over in display flight,
fast and with loudly drumming wings.

Among the ducks are the mallard, the drakes with bottle green head
and the females drab brown. There are tufted duck which feed on small
molluscs found by diving. The ducks are brown, the drakes black and

white. Much smaller are the teal. Again, the females are sober coloured, although very delicately and beautifully marked. The grey and black backed males have chestnut coloured heads marked each side with green.

Ruddy ducks are well established. These bold little birds are familiar throughout the area, the drakes particularly colourful with their white cheek patches and blue bills. Originating from North America, ruddy duck established themselves in the Midlands after escapes from wildfowl collections earlier this century. They appear not have harmed local wildlife, but those which have spread to Spain have begun to hybridise with the local white headed duck and threaten its survival.

To the Trent

Beyond Doxey Marshes the Sow flows past the old Stafford gasworks and derelict Broad Eye windmill, threads its way between buildings, creeps past the flower beds of Victoria Park, sneaks under the bridge in Bridge Street and escapes to the suburbs. At Bridge Street it has travelled 5.25 miles from the confluence of the Meece Brook and fallen 8 metres, a rate of about 1.5 metres per mile. This compares with .2 metres over the previous 5.75 miles.

A riverside footpath enables you to follow the Sow in its level green valley to Baswich where it is joined by the River Penk. In the 1.5 miles from Stafford it has fallen 3 metres, or .8 metres per mile. The augmented river now flows parallel with the Staffordshire & Worcestershire Canal. The valley has narrowed here to about .5 of a mile and between the two waterways are Baswich Meadows, a Site of Special Scientific Interest noted for wet grassland plants.

River and canal stay close for the next 4.25 miles, passing behind Milford village on the edge of Cannock Chase. A little to the north is Tixall gatehouse, a startling Tudor building. If this is the Gatehouse the demolished hall must have been unimaginably grand. It is now managed by Landmark Trust as a rather spectacular holiday home.

The Sow runs alongside Shugborough Park which we mentioned in the section on the River Trent, and here the Sow empties into the Trent at the historic Essex Bridge.

Towns and their rivers;

above; the Sow at Doxey Marshes Nature Reserve, Stafford

left; the Trent at Burton

River Blithe

Staffordshire's cleanest river

The Staffordshire Blithe rises at 280 metres near Cellarhead about
5 miles east of Stoke on Trent. It avoids towns and flows through
only one substantial village, maintaining Grade B quality for
almost its whole length.

The first mile or so runs through upland pasture then trickles into
Creswell's Piece, an extensive hillside pasture woodland where cattle
graze under old oak trees. The soil is acidic encouraging the growth
of bilberry, which is attractive to green hairstreak butterflies.

In Creswell's Piece the Blithe merges with another small stream
before crossing the road at Sheepwash. More headwaters join from
the west at Roughcote before the infant river skirts the fringes of
Stoke on Trent at Weston Coyney. Flowing through the narrow rural
gap between Meir and Caverswall, the Blithe runs close to the 17th
century castellated mansion that stands on the site of the 13th
century Caverswall Castle.

A mile or so further on is Blythe Bridge, an expanding village more
or less joined to Stoke-on-Trent. At this point the Blithe has flowed
about 5 miles from its source and fallen 110 metres, a rate of 22
metres per mile. It now levels off.

The river sneaks through the centre of Blythe Bridge past the station
and under the A50 to reach fields. It begins to swell as four small
tributaries join, passes a factory at Cresswell and flows beside the
Stoke - Derby railway for 2.5 miles. To the south-west are the
remains of moats at Paynsley Hall and Blithewood Moat.

North of the railway some fields round Blythe House Farm were
discovered a few years ago to be rich in wild flowers. They had been
managed in a traditional way without the use of herbicides, so were
shining examples of the type of meadows once found all over the
country. Then someone proposed a service station on part of the
land, which increased its speculative value. The land changed hands
and although the service station was never built, the agriculture
intensified and many of the wild flowers are gone. Nothing could
be done because none of the changes needed planning permission.

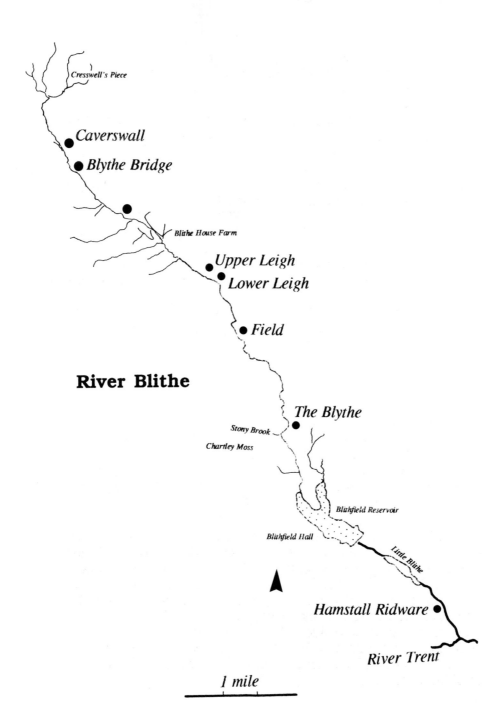

Cresswell's Piece

Caverswall

Blythe Bridge

Blithe House Farm

Upper Leigh

Lower Leigh

Field

River Blithe

The Blythe

Stony Brook

Chartley Moss

Blithfield Reservoir

Blithfield Hall

Little Blithe

Hamstall Ridware

River Trent

1 mile

Hamlets & meadows

The river continues to twist and turn close to the railway through this quiet valley to reach the Leighs - Upper, Lower, Dods and Church Leigh. The church in Church Leigh stands on top of the hill near the centre of the village and overlooking the river.

At Lower Leigh the Blithe has flowed 4.4 miles from Blythe Bridge and fallen 44 metres, a rate of 10 metres per mile. The next section again levels off to half the previous rate. Here it changes course away from the railway and heads south for Field. Little more than a hamlet, Field lies just to the east of the river which continues to meander quietly through pastures.

This is an area of hamlets, the river next coming close to Gratwich. Mentioned in Domesday book when it belonged to Robert of Stafford, it was a big settlement in those days. The brick church of St Mary was built in 1775 since when it has become home to a colony of bats.

Six sluices once let water from the river to flood the King's Field, and it was a common way of managing meadows. Silt from the river enriched the soil and the flowing water did not freeze, allowing grass to get a head start early in the year. Nearby where the river passes beneath the A518 is Burndhurst Mill, which still ground animal feed until the 1950s.

The river continues south through green fields which gently rise and fall and passes under the disused Stafford to Uttoxeter railway. About a mile on it reaches The Blythe, another small hamlet clustered around an inn. It seems strange that the settlements spell their names differently from the river, but standard spelling is an eighteenth century idea.

At The Blythe the river channel divides and several other streams join, creating a watery, willowy landscape. The Stony Brook flows in from the west just beyond the A518 where it has cut a valley beneath the ruins of Chartley Castle. In recent years the valley's future has been threatened by proposals to fill it up with rubbish. This brilliant idea sounds like vandalism and would destroy a pleasant area of countryside. However we doubt whether the National Rivers Authority would permit it because of the effect on water quality, given that the Blithe is just about to form a drinking water reservoir.

Chartley Moss

Just south of the Stony Brook and only half a mile from the Blithe is Chartley Moss, one of the most amazing places in the Midlands. The Moss is a National Nature Reserve originating when the ice carved out a deep, steep sided lake. Over thousands of years the surface was colonised by vegetation which formed a floating raft. There are few nutrients here, so the vegetation includes insect-eating plants like sundews which live by catching flies, rather than getting nutrients from the soil.

Over time, the raft at Chartley was colonised by trees, particularly Scot's pine. English Nature who manage the site are gradually removing those on the drier areas to protect the primeval atmosphere and the wildlife. Where the trees seed onto the floating bog they grow for a few years until their size and weight increases. Slowly they sink until their roots become waterlogged and the trees die. Many fall through the raft into the black, peaty depths. Sometimes gases working beneath the surface send long dead trees back up through the raft, to stand like memorials to their dead cousins.

Chartley Moss is less than half a mile from the main road, yet you could be back in the age of the dinosaurs. It is the best example of a Schwingmoor (floating bog) in Britain, if not Europe. Access is by permit only and by very occasional guided tours which go out across the bog on a floating path of birch and pine logs. Please do not be tempted to go on your own - one step in the wrong direction and you could disappear forever.

Staffordshire's inland sea

From the Stony Brook the Blithe runs south for another 2 miles into Blithfield Reservoir. At this point is has covered 7.5 miles from Lower Leigh and fallen 38 metres, a rate of 5 metres per mile.

People usually approach the reservoir on the B5013 Rugeley - Abbots Bromley road and cross the causeway. Passing the tiny village of Admaston, the road dives down a hill towards what looks like one of the firths on the east coast of northern Scotland. The reservoir at the foot of the hill is set between woods and pasture and is 2.5 miles long and about a mile wide.

Blithfield is a water supply reservoir owned by South Staffordshire Waterworks Company. There are car parks either side of the causeway and you can walk across the dam at the south end. It was first flooded in 1952 and soon discovered by birds so that by 1963 it was rated the third most important reservoir for wildfowl in Britain. The West Midland Bird Club issues permits for bird watching which give access to the shoreline and hides, and you can fish for trout from bank and boat.

The section south-east of the causeway is perhaps the least interesting and has the most artificial appearance due to the vast white dam which crosses this little valley. This area is popular with sailors, but is also the place where in winter you might see rare great northern divers.

North of the causeway the shores are natural, allowing rushes, sedges and other wetland plants to develop. Here the reservoir divides into two long arms, where in dry periods the water falls leaving mudflats which are most attractive to birds.

These northern arms are relatively undisturbed and much favoured by all sorts of birds. Waders such as dunlin, ringed plover, little stint, curlew sandpiper, greenshank, spotted redshank and ruff are attracted by the shallows, with rarer species like Kentish plover and pectoral sandpiper.

Large flocks of wildfowl come in winter - goosander, teal, ruddy duck, mallard and pochard. You can watch cormorants lined up along the water's edge with wings held out to dry. At dusk up to 20,000 gulls fly in to roost from a wide surrounding area. Migrating ospreys often stop here on their way to and from Scotland.

Next to the reservoir is the parkland of Blithfield Hall. In 1367 the manor in which the hall is set passed to the Bagot family who held it until this century. The massive hall has an Elizabethan core but was remodelled in the 19th century.

Each September (on the Monday after the first Sunday after September 4th) the Abbots Bromley Horn Dancers visit Blithefield Hall on their twenty mile circuit of the village. The day long dance starts at dawn and involves performances at the vicarage and throughout the village. There is a hobby horse, Maid Marian, a jester and six deer men, three with black and three with white replica reindeer heads with real antlers. Music is provided by a melodeon player, the hobby horse beats time with its jaws and a bowman twangs his bowstring.

The dance may have prehistoric origins in fertility rites or might be connected with privileges granted to inhabitants of the Forest of Needwood. Anyway, here is an ancient custom living on in 20th century Britain, and it is certainly unique.

On to the Trent

The River Blithe leaves Blithfield Reservoir through the great dam built across the valley. Since entering 2.5 miles back the river has fallen 15 metres, or 6 metres per mile. Soon it divides into two, the northern channel becoming the Little Blithe. The two channels run separately for about 1.5 miles creating a long thin island crossed by a road and three footpaths. Before they meet again the Little Blithe absorbs the Ash Brook from the area of Bagot's Park and flows close to Abbots Bromley.

As the river flows on towards Hamstall Ridware it is paralleled by the Par Brook which rises in Needwood, beyond Newborough and passes close to Hoar Cross. It joins the river behind Hamstall Hall and its surrounding complex of historic buildings. Here it has covered 3.6 miles since the reservoir and fallen another 15 metres, a much reduced rate of 2.7 metres per mile.

The Hall was built in the 16th century for the Fitzherberts on a quadrangle plan in brick with stone dressings, but is now in ruins by the farmhouse. Nearby is the Tudor gatehouse, more or less complete with two capped turrets flanking an arch, and there is a ruined watchtower. St Michael church is of Saxon and Norman origins but rebuilt since the 14th century.

From Hamstall Ridware it is only a mile before the River Blithe empties its waters into one of the branches of the River Trent at King's Bromley. In this short distance the Blithe falls 4 metres or so, making a steep finish.

River Tame

The Legacy

The River Tame has two arms which rise about 7.5 miles apart. The northern one runs from about 133 metres at Stow Heath just over a mile south-east of Wolverhampton. It flows, or trickles, west and north to Willenhall, then dips south-east to follow the M6 between Walsall and West Bromwich to Bescot, part of Walsall. Here it has travelled 5.5 miles and fallen 23 metres, a rate of about 4 metres per mile.

The Tame's southern arm starts at Blackheath from a source at 175 metres on the foot of Old Hill. This is linked to the very prominent Rowley Hills which form the watershed between Tame and Stour. It heads north through Langley and Oldbury, bears west past Dudley Port and north-east through West Bromwich to Bescot. In 6.5 miles it falls 65 metres, or 10 metres per mile.

The two arms of the river seem to have equal status so we will add both to the distance from Bescot, making a journey to the Trent of about 47 miles.

So far the tiny Tame has passed through a fair sample of one of the most heavily industrialised areas in the world. This environment continues through Birmingham's industrial areas of Saltley, Nechels and Bromford, though there is housing at Castle Bromwich before it reaches open country. At this stage it has been joined by the Rivers Rea and Blythe (including the Cole) so draining most of the conurbation and making the work of the Stour look light.

Apart from collecting sewage effluents, industrial waste water from scores of factories and processes and ordinary urban street run off, the Tame passes beneath two of country's biggest motorway junctions. At Ray Hall the M5 meets M6 and at Spaghetti Junction the A38M meets the M6. Adding to this seepage from contaminated land and old waste tips, probable unattributed discharges from old mine workings and the problems of low flow in dry weather suffered by most urban rivers, it is not surprising that the Tame is the dirtiest river in the region. It starts as Grade E and falls to Grade F for a couple of miles through special purification lakes at Lea Marston. It does emerge much cleaner but does not get out of Grade E.

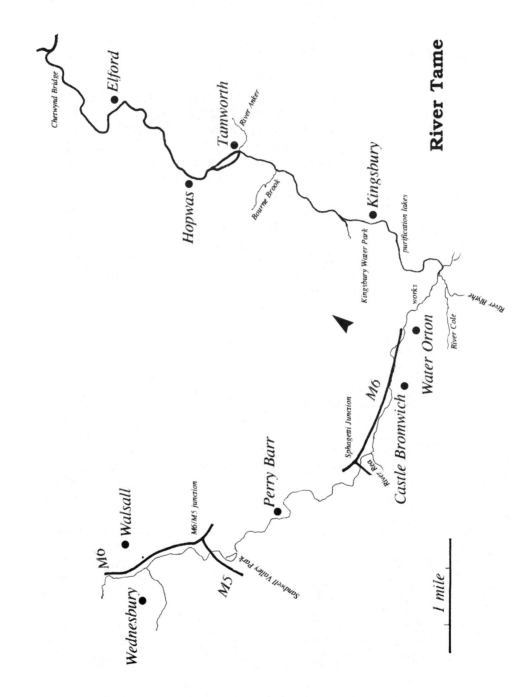

River Tame

*The Tame under the old bridge at Perry Barr,
Birmingham; grey-black and opaque*

*Under Sphagetti Junction; the traffic hamers the ears and the Tame
slithers past unsavoury little islands and drifts of rubbish*

Bescot to Spaghetti Junction

The Tame runs on from Bescot, forming the boundary between the Boroughs of Walsall and Sandwell, and continues beneath the Ray Hall motorway junction. Immediately south is the more open and interesting Sandwell Valley which contains one of the few urban reserves run by the Royal Society for the Protection of Birds. Surrounded as it is by the conurbation, the reserve plays a vital role in educating children about wildlife and providing a haven for numerous birds.

Swan Pool, the centrepiece of the reserve, was drained when the M5 was built but later re-flooded and expanded. Other new pools were created and woods planted. At least 120 species of birds may be seen including swallow, tree pipit, yellow wagtail and even the occasional rarity like Caspian tern. Lapwing and snipe enjoy the damp hollows.

Another stream joins the river having first passed through the Fish Pond on Handsworth Golf Course. At Hamstead the Tame serves a mill pond and passes through Cherry Orchard Recreation Ground en route for Perry Hall Playing Fields. Here there is a link to the moat before the river passes the greyhound track and heads for Perry Bridge on the Aldridge Road.

Reaching the M6 again, the Tame turns more or less south to Witton and under the Aston Expressway near the magnificent Aston Hall. It runs on for about 3 miles beneath the M6 viaduct and past Fort Dunlop to Junction 5. At Spaghetti Junction The Tame has travelled 7.3 miles from Ray Hall and fallen 10 metres at 1.37 metres per mile, a radical levelling.

The River Rea

Most major cities have a river which provided the first inhabitants with water and possibly transport. But Birmingham was created by the Industrial Revolution for different reasons and there is no big river.

The Rea is a 12 mile stream that creeps through the city unseen to join the Tame near Spaghetti Junction. It is one of the many small rivers rising on the Clent and Lickey Hills which run to the Severn, Avon and Trent. From a series of streams around Rubery and Frankley at about 220 metres, the first few rural yards come to an abrupt end at the Longbridge Car Plant. Nearby it flows through Daffodil Park before heading on to Northfield Recreation Ground and Wychall Reservoir.

Skirting the reservoir it comes to King's Norton Park, then heads for Stirchley, passing on the way mill ponds and mill races, evidence of the days when even the Rea worked for industry. On through Selly Park, there are playing fields to Cannon Hill Park, then the Rea skirts the Edgbaston cricket ground and passes through Calthorpe Park to the city centre.

The Rea is channelled and culverted but cuts a clear and quite green route between the buildings. Later housing developments have left the valley as open space and it now forms a walking and cycling route between the Longbridge area and Highgate.

Passing under Mill Road, Duddeston, the Rea arrives at Nechells and a conglomeration of gas holders, power stations and pumping stations. Nearby, the roar of M6 and Aston Expressway points to an insalubrious end for this most urban of rivers. Water quality is Grade E. The Rea falls 120 metres, but it drops 70 metres in the first mile and 50 metres in the 11 urban miles, a rate of only 4.5 metres per mile.

The Tame to Hams Hall

At last the Tame is temporarily free of motorways as it heads for the massive Minworth Water Treatment Works. This enormous complex now processes most of the sewage for the conurbation, which may sound like bad news for the Tame, but this is far from the truth.

One of the problems which has dogged the river for many years is the poor standard of sewage treatment at the many old plants across the built up area. Now much of the waste is pumped to Minworth where modern treatment is finally helping clean up the Tame. We have described in the *Rivers at Work* section how the Tame flows through purification lakes just beyond Minworth at Lea Marston. Essentially they slow the flow and allow suspended solids to settle out. When it leaves the system the river is almost Grade D quality.

Beyond Water Orton is the site of the old Hams Hall Power Stations. When they were working cooling water raised the temperature of the river but that problem has ceased. Now there is to be a Channel Tunnel rail freight terminus, leaving the valuable wetland habitats unscathed. Despite their appearance power station grounds are often surprisingly rich in wildlife. At Hams Hall the West Midland Bird Club manages the Ladywalk Reserve. Apart from about 130 species of birds recorded in most years, the conditions are ideal for plants and butterflies.

Among the breeding waterfowl are those colourful birds more often seen on the coast, shelduck, with commoner species including tufted duck. The gravelly conditions on parts of the site are ideal for little ringed plover and there is a small colony of sand martins.

Apart from water loving birds the common species of warbler are present, with garden warbler, blackcap and sedge warbler. Other birds include spotted flycatcher, treecreeper and nuthatch. Some of the birds use the electrical paraphernalia, with kestrels nesting on pylons and a big rookery over more pylons.

The commoner butterflies such as the small tortoiseshell, peacock and red admiral are abundant, and less common species like the painted lady. Gatekeepers and holly blues do well and there are a few white letter hairstreaks. The wetlands invariably attract dragonflies. Twelve species have been recorded including ruddy darter, common darter and the rare black tailed skimmer.

A highlight of Ladywalk is the magnificent display of orchids. Hundreds of bee orchids, marsh helleborines and southern marsh orchids like the conditions and so do many hybrids. Other species include a few common spotted and pyramidal orchids.

There are several hides on the reserve and bird feeding stations. Access is by permit only from the West Midland Bird Club.

Along the Blythe

At Hams Hall, the Tame is joined by the somewhat cleaner Blythe from the south (Grade D) and small River Bourne from the east. The Blythe is about 24 mile long but falls only 95 metres. Some 47 metres of this occurs in the first 5 miles, an initial rate of over 9 metres per mile. The Blythe is formed from several tributaries. The main two

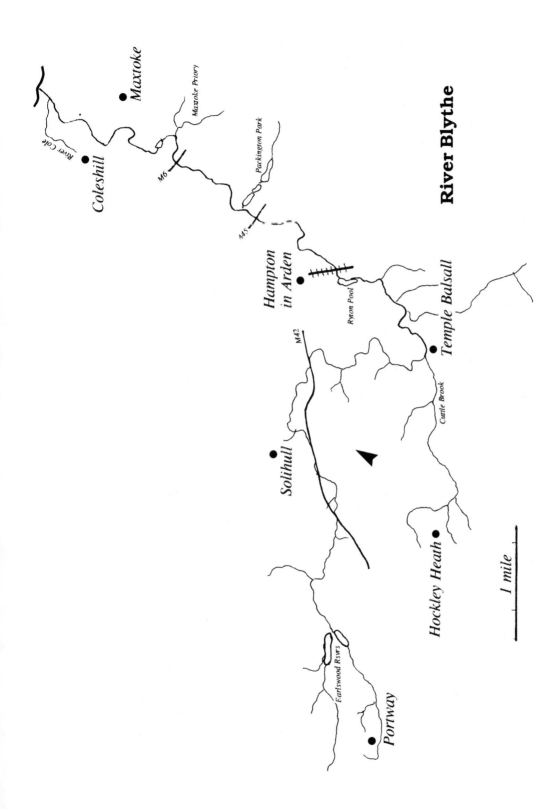

River Blythe

Coleshill

River Cole

Maxtoke

Maxtoke Priory

M6

A45

Packington Park

Hampton in Arden

Ryton Pool

Temple Balsall

Curtle Brook

M42

Solihull

Hockley Heath

Portway

Earlswood Rsws

1 mile

rise around Forshaw Heath, near junction 3 of the M42 and both flow to Earlswood Lakes, which are reservoirs for the Stratford upon Avon Canal.

This short section of the Blythe is no better than Grade C. Earlswood Lakes suffer from algae which increases biochemical oxygen demand, but at present water quality remains Grade C and this is generally the case almost to the Tame.

From the lakes the river passes beneath the canal, passes Cheswick Green and dives under the M42, which follows the river valley for about 2 miles towards Solihull. The river wriggles close to the town and picks a tributary from Tudor Grange Park, but turns away south-east towards Barston, runs under the Grand Union Canal and M42 again to pass the Water Treatment Works.

Looping south towards Temple Balsall, the Blythe is joined by several streams from the south which rise near the National Trust's Packwood House and Baddesley Clinton. They flow through a gentle, agricultural landscape and alongside the Grand Union Canal.

From Temple Balsall the Blythe heads north again, gaining in size all the time to pass Barston Water Treatment Works. Ammonia from this works has been one of the river's major problems. Passing under the Birmingham - Coventry railway at Hampton in Arden, it reaches Stonebridge and Packington Park.

This area is the Meriden Gap, a corridor of open country between Birmingham, Solihull and Coventry which planners are anxious to preserve. It thunders under the burden of main roads and railways with the M42 up the middle, and has been bitten at by Birmingham Airport and the National Exhibition Centre. The River Blythe and the Heart of England Way Long Distance Footpath run through it like mute protests.

North of the A45 and the M6, the Blythe meanders through a level and fairly featureless landscape with the fringe of the conurbation less than a mile to the west. Lacking the rises, falls and essential prettiness of the Meriden Gap, it seems a landscape deserted by people and lost to motorways, railways and huge stalking pylons. But there are traces of a rural past. Footpaths cross the river on little bridges, there are a couple of fords, there is Maxstoke Mill and at one time someone was pleased to build Blythe Hall on the bank about a mile from the Tame.

Within 500 yards of the Tame the river Cole joins from the west. With the Rea, this is the third of the conurbation's urban rivers which drain into the Tame and Trent. The Tame, Rea and Cole are wholly urban, the Blythe a little less so but the water quality is only a Grade better.

Along the Cole

This little river rises near the Blythe, it is about as long, has much the same fall and water quality varies from C to D. We will not describe it all but there are points of interest.

Sarehole Mill between the suburbs of Springfield and Hall Green was built in the 1760s. It was in use as a corn mill until 1919, then decayed to the point of demolition until 1960, when it was rescued by Birmingham City Council. It is open during the summer and demonstrates flour grinding. The red brick mill is dominated by its chimney, hinting at the steam engine which was installed to supplement the water power.

The countryside which surrounded the mill in the early 1900's inspirated Tolkein's books *The Hobbit* and *Lord of the Rings*. Tolkein enthusiasts will know that the mill features in the saga. Sorry to be vague but we found it rather hard to get on with. Just upstream of the mill is Trittiford Mill Pool and, unusually in an urban setting, a ford in Scriber's Lane.

The second point of interest on the Cole is the recent history of Moseley Bog, which we offer to encourage people to fight for their own green spaces. In the early 1980s developers put up a planning proposal to build twenty two houses on part of Moseley Bog, just a few hundred yards from Sarehole Mill. The Bog was once part of a much larger marsh called Greet Common which was fed by a 2 mile tributary of the River Cole, the Coldbath Brook.

In the 18th century the Brook fed four pools. All were fish ponds harvested by nets and all except one were on common land. Old Pool on the site of Moseley Bog was a reservoir for Sarehole Mill. Less water was needed from the 19th century and the meadow below the Old Pool became waterlogged, probably because the dam leaked. Eventually the pool was drained, but the land was never reclaimed. Some drainage was done in the 1950s when part of the area was used for playing fields, but a good area remained wet meadow, rich in wild flowers.

The threat to Moseley Bog galvanised local people who formed a "Save Our Bog" group. They mounted a big campaign demonstrating the site's wildlife value, importance for education and local amenity value. The planning application was refused, the protestors became the Friends of Moseley Bog and, working with the Wildlife Trust, eventually had the bog declared a Local Nature Reserve.

On its way north and east the Cole threads its way past the Tyseley Railway Museum, under the A45 at Hay Mills, and through Stechford, Shard End, Tile Cross and Chemlsley Wood. All the way it links a string of recreation grounds and green spaces. This river corridor has been promoted and enhanced for many years by Project Kingfisher, which has improved the environment and created a series of woods and meadows.

The National Rivers Authority has drafted a Catchment Management Plan for the Rivers Blythe, Cole and Bourne, (We have mentioned CMP's for the Black Country Stour and the Avon.) The plans examine local water uses which affect river quality and note the important issues. On the Blythe and its tributaries these include algae on Earlswood Lakes, ammonia from Barston Sewage Works, wildfowl pollution from a an ornamental lake in Solihull, sewage pollution from a recreation ground, chemical pollution from the de-icer at Birmingham Airport, high nitrates in the River Bourne and urban development. They are typical of the problems suffered by urban and urban fringe rivers.

The Tame to Tamworth

Beyond Hams Hall and on the east bank of the river is the Warwick-shire Wildlife Trust's Nether Whitacre reserve. It was once part of a sand and gravel quarry and marks the start of several miles of flooded workings.

This reserve is a dense thicket of willow and alder scrub around wet grassland and pools. The scrub is not good for plants but provides shelter for birds like the reed warbler, sedge warbler and water rail. There are many insects including the banded agrion damselfly. The grassland contains a good selection of wild flowers, including the common centaury, common spotted orchid and marsh orchid.

For the next half mile the Tame passes through the Lea Marston purification lakes which we have already described. Skirting some further lakes, it passes Kingsbury high on the east bank. At the brick footbridge the river is full and fast and tumbles over some rocks, but as you might expect from its experience, it has a steely, dead look and a raw, dank smell.

On the valley floor to the west are most of the old gravel pits which now form Kingsbury Water Park. They were abandoned in 1973 after 50 years working had left 600 acres of the Tame valley as a series of huge holes separated by narrow necks of ground. Some had been filled with ash from Hams Hall Power Station but most had brimmed naturally with water. Warwickshire County Council took over the site as a public amenity, encouraged natural colonisation by mosses, grasses, reeds, willows, brambles, birch, alder and oak, made some additional plantings and laid out paths and tracks. There are 30 pools and many of the secluded fishing waters are quite small. However the three largest lakes each cover about 60 acres. You can sail full size or model boats, windsurf, fish, watch birds, orienteer, ride horses, picnic, camp, caravan, stroll or collapse in a heap.

In the next 2 miles the Tame flows north and the land to the east becomes a little higher and more hilly. Although disguised by the urban area to the south of Tamworth, this is the northern tip of the small range west of the River Anker which overlooks Nuneaton and Atherstone. To the west, the flatness of the Trent valley gives way over 2 or 3 miles to slightly higher land at Sutton Coldfield and an amazing outcrop of baby alps at Weeford.

Around the north of these comes the fast flowing Black Brook from Shenstone which joins the Bourne Brook, and from them come the network of waterways around Fazeley. The Brook runs through Drayton Manor Park, once the property of Robert Peel where it served the fish ponds and duck decoy. Immediately beyond Fazeley it enters the Tame.

Along the Anker

The Tame flows into Tamworth under the ring road and is joined beneath the castle by the River Anker. This 24 mile river rises as a series of streams about 5 miles south-east of Nuneaton. We should probably say ditches; on the maps they are fine straight lines around the edges of fields.

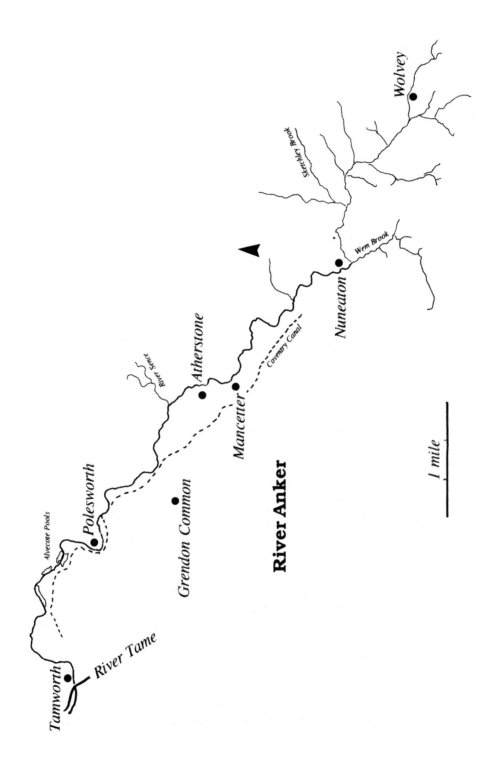

River Anker

1 mile

The Anker falls only 57 metres, an average of .4 metres per mile, and it starts on so slight a fall at .36 of a metre for the first 2 miles that we wonder it gets started at all. It is unlike all other rivers in this book in that its fall is lowest at the sources and increases near its mouth to 1.3 metres per mile.

The water quality of the Anker starts at Grade B but falls to C before it enters Nuneaton. This is generally maintained as it runs through the middle of the town, then north of Atherstone and past arable farmland and old industrial sites to Tamworth. Its Tributaries are more remotely rural and generally quite clean.

Nuneaton was a market town which became a mining centre but there are ancient traces. A wealthy order of Benedictine nuns set up a priory by the Anker in the 12th century and the ruins can be seen near the church of St. Mary which incorporates some of its walls.

From Nuneaton the Anker heads north-west in the same valley as the Coventry Canal, the Tamworth - Coventry railway line and the A5. In fact they continue more or less parallel to Tamworth. Passing the small village of Caldecote, the river stays to the south of the A5 as far as Mancetter.

The Anker passes Mancetter and Atherstone to meet its main tributary, the River Sence at King Dick's Hole. This may refer to Richard III who was killed in August 1485 at the Battle of Bosworth Field some 5 miles east.

The Anker runs on through Bradley Green and Polesworth and under the M42 before flowing through the Warwickshire Wildlife Trust's reserve at Alvecote Pools. This 550 acre Site of Special Scientific Interest is leased from British Coal and has been managed by the Trust since 1959. A series of subsidence pools left by coal mining form a valuable habitat for aquatic plants, insects and birds.

Both the canal and railway at Alvecote were built to carry the coal and there is a massive spoil heap near the M42. This is part of the reserve and has some features of interest but is all too popular with motorbike scramblers. You can get a booklet about the reserve from the Trust, and beside it the County Council have set up a picnic area.

At Amington the river leaves the Coventry Canal to head for the centre of Tamworth through a large triangle of green land. This stretch of river demonstrates the Anker's exceptionally slow flow, sometimes barely moving at all, which has encouraged much wildlife and many plants and animals more typical of ponds.

Tamworth

Tamworth is a small town with a long and rich history and can claim to have been capital of England twice, which is more than London. From 757 to 796 Tamworth was the seat of King Offa and capital of the Kingdom of Mercia. As he was overlord of England, Tamworth was virtually capital of the whole country. Offa's palace was very probably in the area of Market Street, and Tamworth continued to be a royal residence until burned by the Danes in 874, when Mercia ceased to be an independent kingdom.

In 924 Athelstan again established a royal residence in the town. His sister Editha married the Danish king of Northumbria, Sitgtryg, but the marriage soon failed. [What do you expect if you marry someone called Sitgtryg?] She established Tamworth as England's smallest borough. Anyway, enough of the history.

In 1965 Tamworth was designated to take a good part of the overspill population of Birmingham. Acres of modern housing form sprawling suburbs and the town has one of the highest population densities of any in Britain. There is limited open space so the council have tried to leave green wedges linking the centre with the countryside. These are particularly noticeable where they follow the river corridors and can be quite spectacular when floods attract birds to the riverside meadows.

This partly explains why Tamworth's urban area is shaped like a dumbell with the centre in a very short handle. Here are the shops, the castle, the gardens, and the place where where the Anker joins the River Tame. The green reach of the Anker mentioned above is the reason for the gap to the north-east and we hope it will be preserved. However there are development plans as the town fills the land within the Borough boundary.

Tamworth is not so famous for its mute swans as Stratford upon Avon but usually there are more of them. Herds on the Tamworth waterfront are a popular attraction and among the best studied swans in the country. Local naturalist Bert Coleman has been studying swans in Staffordshire and Birmingham for around a quarter of a century and is a recognised authority. Many of the birds wear leg rings so Bert and his helpers can track their movements. Each year they round up the swans to ring new ones and check their health and condition.

Tamworth's meadows are one of only a dozen places in England where the snake's head fritillary grows wild. This delicate member of the lily family sends forth its drooping, cup shaped chequered pink or white flowers every April to delight the privileged few who care for them. The fritillary meadow has been managed to protect the plants for more than twenty years and is on private land with no public access. However, the Staffordshire Wildlife Trust is working with the Borough Council to secure the meadow as a nature reserve.

Tamworth to the Trent

The Anker joins the Tame at Lady Bridge as the Tame enters a wide green area called Broad Meadow. Here it splits in two, with a weir letting into a flood relief channel just south of the main stream. It returns a mile downstream over another weir.

The Tame turns north under the A51 at the red sandstone Hopwas Bridge and runs parallel with the Birmingham and Fazeley Canal beside Hopwas Hays Wood. This big deciduous woodland is mentioned in our previous book, *Midland Woods & Forests*. Although largely a training area for troops from Whittington Barracks, there are public rights of way. It is one of the biggest, densest thickets of birch we have ever seen.

Tamworth and Hopwas Hayes Wood can be seen as areas of higher ground standing like gateposts at the end of the Tame valley, for here the Tame enters the huge, flat plain of the Trent. However, the higher ground continues north-east as the edge of the Trent valley and the Tame follows it to Elford. The A513 from Tamworth crosses a high shoulder on the way to the village and gives big views of the Tame, sweeping to and fro through level fields some 18 metres below. The river is now big and powerful and not much smaller than the Trent.

A little nearer Elford, which is a delightful riverside village, there are two bridges carrying a minor road over the Tame. The larger stone structure is pleasant enough, but the older brick bridge with its irregular arches is delightful. Oddly, it has a pond beneath but no river, suggesting an old channel.

Just to the south of the river are the gravel workings and old pools around the stately Fisherwick Hall. Despite the evidence of the gravel industry all around, this is a quiet area rich in bird life. Thanks to a public footpath passing between the pools much of it can easily be seen

In its last 5 miles gravel pits line the Tame highlighting the importance of this area for producing aggregate. By the steel lattice Chetwynd Bridge, one of the larger and more regular shaped old pits has been formed into a recreation lake, whilst others are unofficial nature reserves. This is the area where both ringed and little ringed plovers nest, their eggs perfectly camouflaged against the shingle.

By Water Orton's beautiful sandstone bridge
the Tame receives the outfall from the vast
Minworth Sewage Works

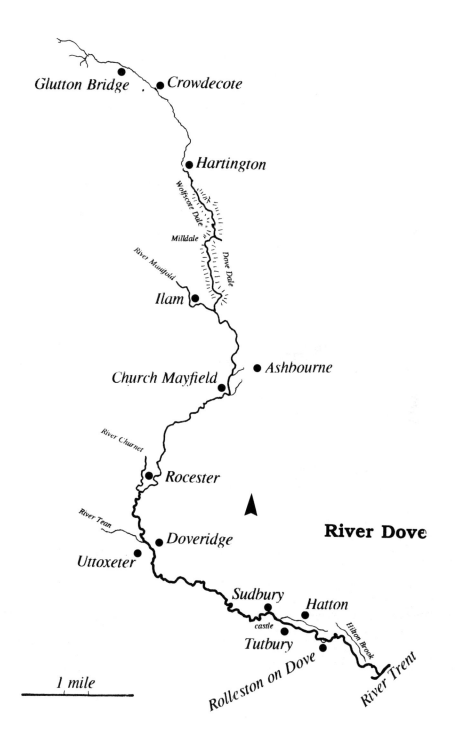

Glutton Bridge

Crowdecote

Hartington

Wolfscote Dale

Milldale

Dove Dale

River Manyfold

Ilam

Ashbourne

Church Mayfield

River Churnet

Rocester

River Tean

Doveridge

Uttoxeter

River Dove

Sudbury

Hatton

castle

Tutbury

Hilton Brook

Rolleston on Dove

River Trent

1 mile

River Dove

Moorland & gorges

The Dove rises on the gritstone moors about 3 miles south of Buxton. Here several streams meet at about 400 metres and race down a deep, steep limestone valley to Glutton Bridge. After 3.8 miles the Dove has fallen 220 metres, or 58 metres per mile. This is the sharpest drop of any river in the book, including the Severn and Teme. For the next 5.5 miles to the village of Hartington, the fall is another 45 metres, a rate of 8.3 metres per mile. This rushing upland water through limestone country is Grade A quality, and two grades cleaner than any other Trent river.

From Hartington water quality remains Grade A and the river tumbles on. Under Wolfscote Hill the Dove is squeezed into the narrow gorge of Wolfscote Dale and wooded Dovedale, one of the most beautiful areas in the country. This is the river favoured by Izaak Walton in his book *The Compleat Angler*. He and his friend Charles Cotton spent much time here and had an ornamental stone fishing lodge built near Beresford Dale.

After almost 7.5 spectacular miles the river reaches the confluence of its large tributary the Manifold. The level is about 130 metres, a fall of 85 metres from Hartington at 11.3 metres per mile.

The Manifold rises some 2.5 miles south of the Dove and flows in a more or less parallel steep sided valley to join the Dove at Ilam, close to the Country Park. The Youth Hostel is in the remains of Ilam Hall which was mostly demolished earlier this century. If this is what is left, just imagine the size of the original building.

The Dove continues south, forming the border between Staffordshire and Derbyshire. It is still an attractive and clean river but its headlong upland career is over. Passing Ashbourne it has fallen only 12 metres in the 3.8 miles from the Manifold, or 3.1 metres per mile. It has started to wind to and fro across a flat bottomed valley about half a mile wide as it heads for Norbury and Rocester.

Rocester has three bridges. East of the village a bridge spans the Dove, on the west another crosses the Churnet. The third provides a link over the mill race which once served the impressive mill.

Excavations at Rocester revealed Roman occupation, but today the main buildings belong to JCB. [Bamford, not Bach.] Surprisingly, the massive factory fronted by wildfowl lakes blends unobtrusively into the surroundings. The village itself is spoilt by some rather inner city looking flats.

Churnet to the Trent

Dove and Churnet share the same valley for a mile before merging. The Dove has travelled some 8.5 miles from Ashbourne and fallen 39 metres, at 4.6 metres per mile the sort of rate we have seen in the middle reaches of many of our other rivers.

Until recently pollution from dye works in Leek reduced the quality of the Grade B Churnet to Grade E for a few miles. However there have been improvements and it now delivers Grade C water to the Dove which is able to continue as Grade B.

Another 2.75 miles and a large tributary, the River Tean, flows in from the west between Uttoxeter and Doveridge. The Dove has fallen only 5 metres from the Churnet confluence at 1.8 metres per mile and its valley is a mile wide and pancake flat. The Dove has started to writhe and meander, a river cutting through soft ground. The high ground which forms the valley's southern edge is the Needwood Plateau, and from the woods on the crest you can see what a major landscape feature the Dove has become.

At Doveridge the fine old stone bridge has thankfully retired in favour of a concrete effort, and despite some modern development the village is a peaceful and rural backwater. It is now more or less bypassed by the A50 and will be completely when the Derby - Stoke link road is complete. St.Cuthbert's church is a solid little building, with stout tower and a short spire in a flowery churchyard that slopes to the river. The churchyard also contains yews so ancient that they are supported by many props. Tradition has it that they are associated with Robin Hood. A track from the church leads to a footpath which crosses the river by a fine suspension bridge. This is apparently the only suspension bridge still in use in Derbyshire and is certainly unexpected on a rural footpath.

Downstream the river passes between Sudbury and Marchington. Footpaths from both villages reach the banks but with no links across, often evidence of a ferry. Sudbury is a quiet, red brick street village, at one end of which is the National Trust's Sudbury

Hall. The Vernons inherited the estate from the Montgomerys and begun building it in 1613.

The Hall has beautiful grounds with a big lake. In spring they are a blaze of golden daffodils and there are views across the river to the Forest of Needwood. The grounds are a remnant of the old deer park which covered 600 acres. The Hall houses a fascinating Museum of Childhood.

From Sudbury, the river twists and turns beneath the ridge of Needwood Forest to Scropton. Although not a village of tremendous historic interest, Scropton is pleasant enough, with a church that looks much older than its hundred or so years. Beyond Scropton the river plunges over a fine weir before another sinuous stretch divides uninspiring Hatton from historic Tutbury.

At Tutbury the river has flowed 11.3 miles from Doveridge and fallen 22 metres at about 2 metres per mile. The rate of fall continues to the Trent at much the same rate, in fact it has hardly changed since the Churnet confluence.

The Mill Fleam which runs around the ramparts of Tutbury Castle served a pond at Tutbury Mill. This was opened in 1783 by John Bott & Co for spinning worsted and cotton. Two 14ft waterwheels powered 7000 spindles and employed 300 people. In 1880 water turbines were installed which remained in use until 1964, although cotton spinning ceased in 1888.

After cotton production ended there was a short period of disuse before J C Staton and Co moved in to make plaster out of gypsum from the nearby Fauld mines. The mill had its own rail link with Tutbury station.

In 1968 the plaster mill closed, the buildings were demolished and the area turned over to a picnic site. By 1993 the Mill Fleam and pond had become heavily silted so the National Rivers Authority and East Staffordshire Borough Council used heavy machinery to clear them. In time vegetation will re-establish and the island will form a haven from dogs and foxes, where waterfowl can nest in peace.

Anglers often line the river bank here, still as willows as they compete with the kingfishers. Among the fish they might catch are chub.

The Dove and Mill Fleam run separately for more than three miles. After the coffee factory at Hatton the scene is dreamily rural. Cows graze the broad meadows around Marston on Dove, where the church seems to stand in a field. Despite the name the village is about half a mile from the river, which has been straightened. The old river now forms a large ox bow lake which has many interesting plants and is a Site of Special Scientific Interest.

Half mile south is Rolleston on Dove, again not actually on the river. Rolleston has become almost a suburb of Burton but keeps its village atmosphere. In Rolleston Spinney is a rookery and a fine lake. Nearby are the grounds of Rolleston Hall which was largely demolished in the 1920s. This was the home of the Mosley family, a member of which was the notorious Sir Oswald Mosley who founded the British Fascist Party.

The valley of the Dove is still marked to the south by the rampart of the Needwood Plateau, but to the north the land hardly rises. The river continues for another couple of miles to be joined by the Hilton Brook. Soon it reaches the A38 bridge - the Roman Ryknild Street, then the historic Monk's Bridge (now a layby), and finally the Trent & Mersey aqueduct. Another mile through willow fringed fields and the Dove empties into the Trent opposite Newton Solney.

Water quality has remained Grade B since the inflow of the Churnet and the Dove is a major water supply river. Pumps at Eggington north of Burton upon Trent send the water to Foremark and Staunton Harold reservoirs to supply the east Midlands. The Dove's clean water confers a major benefit on the Trent, formerly raising it from Grade D to Grade C. Now it helps the Trent to continue so far, accepting the effluents of so many towns, yet remain Grade C.

Further Reading

The Family Water Naturalist, H Angel & P Wolseley, Michael Joseph, 1982

Water Life of Britain, Readers Digest, 1984

Freshwater Life, J Clegg, Warne, 1974

Midland Woods and Forests, J Drewett & J Roberts, Quercus, 1994

Flora of Staffordshire, E S Edees, David & Charles, 1972

Collins Guide to Freshwater Life, R Fitter & R Manuel, Collins

The Birds of the West Midlands, G R Harrison (Ed) West Midland Bird Club, 1982

Life in Lakes and Rivers, T T Macan & E B Worthington, Collins, 1951

Freshwater Fishes, P S Maitland & R N Campbell, Harper Collins, 1992

Taming the Flood, J Purseglove, Oxford University Press, 1988

NRA Catalogue; a list of priced books published by HMSO

Free NRA leaflets on the following in general -

water quality, water supply, farm pollution, oil pollution, pollution from industrial sites, connections to drains, structure, duties and work of NRA.

Free NRA booklets on topics and problems in the Severn Trent region -

Regional Water Rescources Strategy, River Water Quality in the Midlands (1993/4) [a leaflet and a booklet], Objectives for Rivers & Canals (1990), The River Severn, The River Trent, The Severn Bore, Lea Marston Purification Lakes, River Stour Catchment Management Plan Consultation Document (1992), Warwickshire Avon Catchment Management Plan Consultation Summary Report (1994).